SERENDIPITY

SERENDIPITY

Seemingly Random Events, Insignificant Decisions, and
Accidental Discoveries that Altered History

THOMAS J. THORSON

WINDY CITY
PUBLISHERS

SERENDIPITY

Seemingly Random Events, Insignificant Decisions, and
Accidental Discoveries that Altered History

Windy City Publishers
2118 Plum Grove Road, #349
Rolling Meadows, IL 60008
www.windycitypublishers.com

Published in the United States of America

ISBN:
978-1-941478-55-4

Library of Congress Control Number:
2017956655

Cover Design by Stephanie Rocha
stephanierocha.com

WINDY CITY PUBLISHERS
CHICAGO

For my daughters Tierney, Lourdra, and Gilleece,
who inspired me to keep writing,
even though I'm still waiting for them to read
any of the drafts I asked them to review....

Contents

Foreword

FOR AS LONG AS I can remember, I've been fascinated by the vagaries of chance, the "what ifs" that can change the direction of our lives. What if you hadn't gotten lost and asked directions of the woman who would become your wife; what if you hadn't forgotten your car keys and left the house three minutes earlier, so that you would have been crossing the intersection when the drunk driver blew the stop sign; what if the coin flip breaking the stalemate over which college to attend had landed heads instead of tails? Other seemingly insignificant decisions we make every day may have an enormous impact on our lives, but we remain blissfully ignorant of the path open in front of us that quickly closes when we hesitate before stepping outside or turn left instead of right.

In some cases, though, we can trace and ponder the choices we made that brought us to where we are. The genesis of this book arose while driving my daughter to Champaign, Illinois, for her final semester before earning a Master's degree in Teaching English as a Second Language. We looked back at her early interest in anime that bled into an obsession in all things Asian, which led her to enroll in the newly-offered Chinese language course in high school, and then the logical and illogical sequence of events and choices arising out of those decisions that determined her college, major and career, any deviation from which would have completely changed her life's direction. Trying to keep the conversation going as we traveled past endless cornfields, I made casual reference to the remarkable role chance played at one point in history (which turned into the first chapter of this book). She responded with her own example, and we entertained ourselves by speculating as to how the world would be different without the occurrence of random events or accidental happenings. Our trip soon ended, but the idea stuck.

As it turns out, there are any number of turning points in world history that came about by accident, luck, or a random event which tickle the imagination as we speculate how the world would be different if they had not occurred. Would the Civil War have ended differently were it not for a couple of misplaced cigars? Did a wrong turn lead to the deaths of millions of men and women in two world wars? We can also wonder as to the degree of impact these events actually had. Certainly, the accidental discovery of penicillin saved lives, but it is inconceivable that no one at some future time would have developed an antibiotic just as effective, or even penicillin itself. But a delay of just a year or two would have meant a monumental loss of lives in the interim. A husband, mother, or friend would not have survived, not only causing grief to those close to them, but generations of children would never have been born. And as those infants grew into adulthood, how many of them—or how many of their own children or grandchildren or great-grandchildren—made or will make their own discovery that will save lives, or (to be morbid), is there a great evil being among the progeny who would never have been brought into this world?

Which brings all of this discussion down to a very personal level. While it is easy to think that the unlikely event that lit the fuse bringing on World War I is far more significant than the accidental invention of Silly Putty or the chance event that brought Charleze Theron to the screen, how do we really know? Perhaps a couple's first date to *Mad Max* led to romance and marriage, and generations later a child who owes her existence to those nuptials in the distant past will find the secret to curing cancer. Any one of us may exist only because of some chance encounter centuries before. My grandfather's father vehemently opposed the idea of his son leaving the farm to go to college, and only gave in to his wife's insistence long enough to bring him to the train station. Fearful that his father would change his mind, my grandfather boarded the first train to enter the station and enrolled at the first college that had a stop down the line. That led to his meeting my grandmother, who gave birth to my father, which eventually led to me. And now you are reading this book because my nervous grandfather boarded that train.

With each chapter, I hope you are inspired to speculate, daydream, and ponder how, or if, the world would be different on both a global and individual level had it not been for the events related within. Think not only of the immediate impact, but the next-generation permutations. The ripples caused by that butterfly halfway around the world flapping its wings can, after all, be significant indeed.

Image Credits

THE AUTHOR WISHES TO EXTEND his wholehearted thanks to those organizations that dug through their archives to provide images for this work and those that gave permission to use treasured photographs. They are noted below. Where possible, the source of images in the public domain has also been identified. As to all other images not cited below, substantial time and energy has been devoted to determine if any rights were attached or if their use was restricted in any way. If anyone feels that this work is not a fair use of any materials, please contact the author and every effort will be made to respond appropriately. No changes have been made to the original images.

Chapter 1: **1893 | Names in a Hat**
Churchill photo from the collection of the Imperial War Museums, London

Chapter 2: **1936 | Right Side of the Street**

Chapter 3: **1946 | Sticky Pocket**
Image used with permission of Amana Brand

Chapter 4: **1241 | Saved by a Custom**
Mongolian army helmet located in the Tokyo Museum, Kumamoto Prefectural Museum of Art

Chapter 5: **1961 | Strangers on a Train**
Concert photo courtesy of Northfoto/Shutterstock.com

Chapter 6: **Accidental Inventions**
Image courtesy of Andriy Petryna/Shutterstock.com

Chapter 7: **1928 | The Moldy Dish**
Image of poster from the archives of the United States government

Flask and test tube image courtesy of Everett Historical/Shutterstock.com

Chapter 8: **1915 | Missed the Boat**
Photograph provided by and used with the permission of the Eastland Disaster Historical Society

Chapter 11: **Late Thirteenth Century | The Winds of War**
Photograph provided by and used with the permission of *Kyoto News*, Tokyo, Japan

Chapter 12: **Accidental Inventions | Food Edition**
Popsicle® Pops: Images used with permission of the Unilever Group of Companies

Chocolate Chip Cookies: Image courtesy of digital reflections/Shutterstock.com

Chapter 13: **1844 | - .... . / - . -.. . --. .-. .- --. ....**
Image of Morse telegraph key courtesy of Hannes Grobe

Chapter 14: **Famous People Who Eluded Death**
Toscanini: Image of Lusitania from the George Grantham Bain Collection of the Library of Congress

Kern: 1928 promotional image of *Show Boat* originally published in the February, 1928 issue of *Theater Magazine*

Byrd: Photo of young Byrd located in the Prints and Photographs division of the United States Library of Congress, digital ID ggbain.38060

Grant: Publicity photo of Grant pursued by plane in North by Northwest originally published in *Motion Picture Daily*

Ferguson: Image of wedding carriage courtesy of Elke Wetzig

CHAPTER 15: **1862 | THE HAZARDS OF SMOKING**
Image of Order 191 courtesy of Mark A. Wilson

CHAPTER 17: **STARS DISCOVERED PURELY BY CHANCE**
Turner and Wayne: Poster of *The Sea Chase* courtesy of Didier Lasbugas

Monroe: Associated Press photo originally published in the *Corpus Christie Caller Times* on September 16, 1954

CHAPTER 18: **312 A.D. | A SIGN FROM HEAVEN**
Photograph courtesy of Jean-Christophe Benoist

CHAPTER 21: **LUCKY BREAKS THAT MADE CAREERS THAT AFFECTED US ALL**
Reagan: Engagement photo courtesy of the Reagan Library

Lerner and Lowe: Julie Andrews image originally credited to Richard Maney-Photo by Friedman-Abeles, NYC

CHAPTER 22: **DUEL #3: 1864 | THE DUEL THAT NEVER WAS**
Image provided by and used with permission of the Nevada Historical Society

CHAPTER 23: **ACCIDENTAL SCIENTIFIC DISCOVERIES IN THE EARTH AND SKY**
Pompeii: Photograph courtesy of Daniele Florio

Venus de Milo: Photograph courtesy of Mattgirling

Lyceum: Photograph courtesy of Mirjanamimi

Ruins of Serdica: Photograph courtesy of Ann Wuyts

Neanderthal Skeleton: Photograph courtesy of gerasimov_foto_174/Shutterstock.com

Dead Sea Scrolls: Photograph of scrolls courtesy of Ken and Nyetta. Photograph of cave courtesy of Peter van der Sluijs

Coelacanth: Photograph courtesy of Nkanash Rexford

CHAPTER 24: **1914 | A WRONG TURN BRINGS THE WORLD TO WAR**
Photograph of death car in Heeresgeschichtliches Museum courtesy of Ollifoolish

CHAPTER 25: **ACCIDENTAL INVENTIONS | TOY EDITION**
Silly Putty: Photograph courtesy of bigdogLHR

Slinky: Images provided by and used with permission of Alex Brands

CHAPTER 26: **1839 | THAT'S HOW THE (RUBBER) BALL BOUNCES**
Image from the collection of the Library of Congress

CHAPTER 27: **1989 | THE SLIP OF THE TONGUE THAT BROUGHT DOWN A WALL**
Photograph originally taken by the Central Intelligence Agency, United States government

1

1893 | Names in a Hat

THE BRITISH EMPIRE WAS NEVER *so vast as in the Victorian period of the late nineteenth century. It included over sixty territories around the globe, from the tiny Falkland Islands to massive India, measuring more than fourteen million square miles and containing over a quarter of the world's population. The British Navy ruled the seas and a military presence was essential to retaining control of the far-off territories and enforcing the foreign policies of the government. A successful stint as a military officer was a popular choice for an English boy with ambition, as well as a traditional method for one born into noble lineage to bring honor to himself and his family. A distinguished career in the service was also a tried-and-true means of entry into the political arena.*

There were only two military schools in England at the time and entry into either of them required passing a rigorous set of exams, beginning first with a "preliminary exam" taken at the age of 15 or 16. The test covered a variety of subjects, including mathematics, languages, and geography. Failing this initial test would be catastrophic, as only with a passing grade was a boy allowed to continue on to take a school's "further exam," essentially an entrance exam into the military. Prospective students studied with special instructors for six months or more, attempting to gain every advantage on the preliminary exam as if their future depended upon it, which it did.

W. C. was a mediocre student who felt that his instructors contributed little that he didn't already know. He was often "on reports," requiring special oversight of his work by the school, and by his own admission was academically lazy. Like other boys preparing for the exam, he accepted additional instruction, but his habitually poor study habits carried over even then and were an enormous cause for concern. In acknowledgment of his need for a little bit of luck, the night before the exam W.C. resorted to an extraordinary gamble. Every candidate knew that he would be required to draw an accurate map of one of the world's countries; they just didn't know which one. Aware that attempting to cram geographic details of hundreds of nations into his memory in such a short time would be fruitless, W.C. instead wrote the names of every world nation on slips of paper, put them into a hat, and drew one out at random.

The country W.C. selected by chance was New Zealand, so that night he pored over a map of that country to the exclusion of all others. The next day, pencil in hand, he sat down to the test and on the very first question was asked to draw a map of…New Zealand. With more than a little sense of relief, he sketched an uncannily accurate map of both islands, including the locations of cities and rivers. For good measure he added parks, libraries, and even train lines. W.C.'s perfect score on this portion of the test and the confidence he gained in answering the initial question helped him pass the preliminary exam.

He went on to pass the further exam (on his third try) and entered the Royal Military College in Sandhurst in September of 1893, the first step in his military career.

ભ   ભ   ભ

Winston Churchill's military career was undistinguished, but still laid the foundation for his election to the House of Commons in 1901. As a member of Parliament he fought tempestuously to make a name for himself, a strategy that also had the effect of making him unpopular even among some members of his own party. He lost re-election in 1908 but won his seat back again only two years later. In 1914, just as England was on the verge of entering World War I, he was named First Lord of the Admiralty, a post he lost a year later.

Churchill's most important contribution to the history of England and the world was still to come. Out of office in the 1930s, he nevertheless worked to keep himself in the limelight and was a leading voice in warning about the rise of Nazi Germany and in imploring a country reluctant to enter into another war to arm itself. He was an outspoken critic of Prime Minister Neville Chamberlain's policy of appeasement toward Adolf Hitler, but the British government perceived him as a warmongering alarmist and largely ignored him. When Churchill's predictions that Hitler's Nazi movement would spread to threaten all of Europe were borne out and England was forced to declare war on Germany in 1939, he was again appointed to the position of First Lord of the Admiralty, the same post he had held at the outset of World War I.

Winston Churchill visiting bomb-ravaged areas of
the East End of London, September 1940

On May 10, 1940, as Germany began its invasion of France, the English people's confidence in Chamberlain's policies sank to a new low and he resigned. Churchill had positioned himself both politically and in the popular mind as the right person to replace him, and King George VI appointed Churchill prime minister. For the next five years, his stubborn refusal to back down from the powerful forces of the Axis, his courage in the face of a seemingly hopeless situation, and a gift for oratory that inspired the people of Great Britain and beyond would help England hold on until such time as the tide of the war could turn. He is widely credited with leading Great Britain through World War II and being the lynchpin of the coalition that defeated the Axis, and is considered one of the leading statesmen of the twentieth century.

> *...we shall fight in France, we shall fight on the seas and oceans, we shall fight with growing confidence and growing strength in the air, we shall defend our Island, whatever the cost may be, we shall fight on the beaches, we shall fight on the landing grounds, we shall fight in the fields and in the streets, we shall fight in the hills; we shall never surrender."*
>
> ~Winston Churchill, June 4, 1940

2

1936 | Right Side of the Street

CHILDREN LEARNING TO READ IN *the United States in the 1930s had a very limited number of titles to choose from. Most picture books were simply illustrated with a simple storyline to match and contained a moral lesson to impress upon young minds. One of the first and most commercially successful picture books of the time,* Millions of Cats *by Wanda Gág (still in print today), told the tale of an elderly man who set off on a mission to find a cat at the request of his wife. He inadvertently returned with millions of cats. The couple let the cats decide which among them is the prettiest, a vicious contest in which the survivor is a skinny, unassuming cat who never claimed to be pretty at all. He grew fat and happy in the couple's care. The 1930s also saw the introduction of the dull* Dick and Jane *series, which for decades were the books of choice for teaching children across several age groups to read, until the series fell out of favor in the late 1950s.*

During that same period, T.G. had established a successful career as a cartoonist and advertising artist whose work had appeared in over sixty different periodicals and more than a thousand newspapers. Returning from a European vacation, T.G. and his wife booked passage on the Swedish luxury liner M. S. Kungsholm. As they crossed the Atlantic the ship encountered a fierce summer storm that battered the vessel with gale-force winds for days. All the passengers were confined to their cabins to wait out the storm. Claustrophobic and seasick, T.G. passed the time by doodling various versions of a horse and cart he remembered from his childhood. Eventually he began to quietly mutter words to accompany the sketches to the rhythm of "'Twas the Night Before Christmas."

Upon docking in New York, his mind wouldn't let go of the rhythm that had kept him sane through the windy passage, so he set about developing a story around his sketches and the silly words that he'd assigned to them on the ship. Ever the perfectionist, it took him half the year to write and illustrate A Story That No One Can Beat, *in which a boy named Marco prepares to tell his father about the horse and wagon he saw on his walk home but worries that his tale will be too dull. The horse soon becomes a zebra, then a reindeer, then an elephant and finally a brass band; the wagon transforms into a blue-and-gold chariot before further changing into a sleigh as it speeds past a cheering mayor waving banners of red, white, and blue. In the end, mindful of his father's dislike of tales, he relates that all he saw was a mere horse and wagon.*

T.G. was enthusiastic about his story and was surprised by the reactions of publishers he approached. The book flouted the conventions of children's books of the day, he was told, and a fantasy told in verse just wasn't marketable. Worst of all, in T.G.'s mind, was their complaint that the story lacked a moral and was therefore offensive. Twenty-seven times he brought his beloved transcript to a publisher, and twenty-seven times it was rejected.

Walking home from his latest rejection, a desolate T.G. determined that this failure would be his last. Upon returning to his apartment, he planned to ceremoniously burn the tattered manuscript, never to venture into the field of children's literature again. Lost in sad contemplation while making his way home, T.G. was hailed on the street by a classmate who had been a year behind him in college. When asked why he was so glum, T.G. described the lack of success with his book. His tale of woe fell on receptive ears. Just three hours before this chance meeting, his friend had been named editor of juvenile books at Vanguard Press. Half an hour later they were in the Vanguard offices, which enthusiastically agreed to publish the book. The only condition was that the title of the book be changed, to which T.G. agreed.

ଔ ଔ ଔ

And to Think That I Saw It on Mulberry Street by "Dr. Seuss" was an instant success, receiving rave reviews from, among others, the *New York Times* and the *Atlantic Monthly*. Beatrix Potter, of Peter Rabbit fame, called it "the cleverest book I've met with for many a year." Theodor Geisel followed it with *The 500 Hats of Bartholomew Cubbins* and forty-two more titles that he both wrote and illustrated, including *Horton Hears a Who!*, *Green Eggs and Ham*, and *How the Grinch Stole Christmas!*. One of his most successful titles was written in response to a challenge by an editor to write and illustrate a children's primer using only 225 "new reader" words out of a list of 348 such words. The result, of course, was *The Cat in the Hat*. Geisel wrote two dozen more books that were illustrated by other people or written under the pen name Theo LeSieg (and one under the name Rosetta Stone!).

By the time of his death in 1991, Geisel's books had been published in more than twenty languages and had sold over 200 million copies, a figure that has continued to grow. A listing of the 100 top-selling children's books of all time in *Publisher's Weekly* in the year 2000 contained no fewer than sixteen Dr. Seuss titles. His long-lasting popularity is a testament to his imagination and ability to enchant children with silly verses and irreverent illustrations, but the books may never have existed if not for a chance meeting on a New York street. As Geisel himself once said, "If I had been going down the other side of the Madison Avenue, I'd be in the dry-cleaning business today."

"Jane said, "Run, run.
Run, Dick, Run.
Run and see."

~Fun with Dick and Jane

"But all that I've noticed, Except my own feet
Was a horse and a wagon on Mulberry Street.
That's nothing to tell of,
That won't do, of course....
Just a broken-down wagon
That's drawn by a horse.
That can't be my story. That's only a start.
I'll say that a ZEBRA was pulling that cart!
And that is a story that no one can beat,
When I say that I saw it on Mulberry Street.
Yes, the zebra is fine,
But I think it's a shame,
Such a marvelous beast
With a cart that's so tame.
The story would really be better to hear
If the driver I saw there were a charioteer.
A gold and blue chariot's something to meet,
Rumbling like thunder down Mulberry Street.

~And to Think That I Saw It on Mulberry Street

3

1946 | Sticky Pocket

THE GENERAL PRINCIPLE OF COOKING *hasn't changed for millennia: apply heat to raw food. For thousands of years, this meant using an open wood fire, either by placing food directly into or above the flames, or by use of a cauldron of some sort for soups and stews. Although the ancient Greeks reportedly used a form of oven for baking, the first clear predecessor of the modern stove was built in Alsace, France in 1490. Composed of brick and tile, it was the first design that incorporated a flue. Nevertheless, no consideration had been given to the smoke produced by the burning wood and the concept did not immediately catch on.*

It wasn't until the early 1700s that the Germans introduced the next innovation in home cooking, the cast-iron oven. Over in the American colonies, brick beehive-shaped ovens were all the rage. In either case, the only way to regulate the heat was through the amount of wood used, and the cook's only method of testing the temperature of the oven was to place his or her hands inside. Wood was still the fuel of choice, although that would soon be changing. In 1833, a man by the name of Jordon Mott invented the first practical coal oven, which was ventilated to improve the efficiency of the burn. The use of coal remained limited until late in that century, when the growth of coal and iron mining made possible an expanded use of cast iron to make the stove with coal as its source of heat.

Around the same time, creative minds turned to the use of natural gas in place of wood. The gas stove appeared as early as 1802, although the first commercially produced model appeared in Britain when it was patented by inventor James Sharp in 1826. By the early 1900s, in great part due to the spread of gas lighting, gas ovens were found in most households in the United States. Electric ovens were invented in the 1880s, but did not provide practical competition for gas for about forty more years. Gas and electric have been the mainstays ever since.

For the modern style of most stoves, with an oven below and a flat-topped range on top, we can thank Benjamin Thompson, who also went by the name of Count Rumford. Thompson's studies of heat transfer while perfecting methods for boring cannons in the 1790s led him to design a stove whose design was the forerunner of those still in use today. His genius, as one source noted, was "to take cooking fire out of the open hearth and put it in a box." The top of the stove contained round holes of different sizes that opened to the fire below; the cook would lower specially-designed pots and pans to the desired height above the flame. The Count's other claim to fame, also still in use today, is the Thermos bottle.

The year 1910 found ovens displaying the classic form of two burners on top with an oven and a broiler at the bottom. Subsequent years expanded the number of burners as more reliable methods of regulating the heat on stovetops were invented. After that, the designers took over. Stoves lost their legs, gained gadgets such as timers and custom controls, and began to appear in a number of decorative colors. The cook of the 1940s made meals on or in these new fancy appliances, but the concept was the same as it had always been: apply heat to raw food.

Enter Percy Spencer. Despite having little formal education as a child, Spencer took an intense interest in electronics and how things worked. At the age of 14, he was hired to install electricity at a paper mill. Inspired by the heroics of the radio operators on the Titanic, he enlisted in the Navy as a way of learning more about this relatively new form of technology. While on night watch, he furthered his education even more by reading every textbook he could lay his hands on. Following his discharge and the end of World War I, Spencer took a job at a new firm called American Appliance Company, which later changed its name to Raytheon Manufacturing Company; it specialized in the design and production of weaponry. Spencer soon became one of the company's most valuable engineers and was its go-to problem solver. During World War II, he developed proximity fuses that allowed a soldier to trigger artillery shells to explode in mid-air prior to hitting their mark.

Eventually his primary focus was on finding more efficient and effective ways to mass-produce radar magnetrons, a type of electric whistle that creates vibrating electromagnetic waves instead of sound waves. For a period in 1946, he was attempting to increase the power level of magnetron tubes used in radar sets. While testing one of his magnetrons, Spenser put his hand into his pocket, expecting to pull out a peanut cluster bar for a snack. What he found instead was a sticky mess. The peanut bar had melted. Curious as to what had happened, he ran another test with a magnetron by sticking an egg underneath the tube. Moments later, it exploded and he literally had egg on his face. The following day he brought corn kernels to work and popped them in his magnetron. The microwave oven was born.

CR   CR   CR

The next year, in 1947, Raytheon built the first commercially available microwave oven, called the Radarange. It was a powerful machine with the ability to cook a six-pound roast in two minutes. Standing over five feet tall and weighing in at nearly 750 pounds, and with a price tag of over two thousand dollars, it was not an immediate success. Efforts by Tappan Stove Company to market a microwave in the 1950s met with a similar fate, again due to cost. It was only after Raytheon acquired Amana and introduced a countertop model in 1967 that the microwave oven began to find its way into American homes. As technological advances made the microwave more affordable and more companies entered the market, Spencer's invention became a household essential. Today, ninety percent of homes in the United States contain a microwave oven.

Make the greatest cooking discovery since fire.

~Amana Radarange advertising, 1968

Radarange advertisement from 1968

4
1241 | Saved by a Custom

I N THE EARLY PART OF *the thirteenth century, the Mongols consisted of a number of tribes roaming around parts of central and northern Asia, each tribe content to exist independent of the others with occasional warring amongst themselves. A fierce warrior named Temujin, through both skilled diplomacy and success in battles with other clans, rose to prominence. As his strength grew, he executed the leaders of other tribes and anyone who resisted him, eventually being recognized as the leader of the Mongolian region with equal measures of fear and reverence. In the year 1206, Temujin took the title of Universal Ruler, that is, Genghis Khan.*

Although today his name is associated with ruthlessness in battle, one of Genghis Khan's greatest accomplishments was to unify the various Mongol tribes into one powerful nation. Early in his rule, he enacted the Yasa, a set of laws and moral codes affecting every aspect of Mongol life, including purity laws, rituals of sacrifice, and laws regarding murder, theft, and divorce. Equally as important, he believed that it was his religious duty to unify the world and to bring all people under the aegis of the Mongols and for all to submit to the laws of the Yasa. Just as there was only one god in heaven, so there should be only one empire on earth. And so began one of the greatest sets of conquests the world has ever known.

The Mongol army was a fighting force unlike any that had come before it. Hunting parties became clinics in battle strategy and allowed young men to sharpen their skills with weapons on animals before using them on other men. Their archers, using bows more powerful than those of their foes, were the most skilled marksmen of their time. The cavalry's horsemanship was unparalleled and the foot soldiers were highly disciplined. Unlike other armies who favored heavy armor, the Mongol warriors wore light armor that offered extreme maneuverability. An elaborate system of communication through the use of flags, torches, and riders provided constant communication with a central command during battle. They were fast, seemingly fearless, and vicious in battle. Just as important, the Mongol leaders were ingenious strategists, often winning battles in which they were vastly outnumbered by outsmarting opposing generals.

The Mongols first marched to the East and into China, winning battle after battle. Following these early successes, Genghis Khan soon turned his eyes to the west. In 1219, the warriors swept across eastern Europe and the areas that are now Afghanistan, Iraq, Iran, and Turkey. Everywhere they went, they spread death and destruction. Entire cities were destroyed. Any captive that could be used was spared; all others were killed. It was almost too easy. In the words of one historian, they "completely outclassed, outfought, and utterly defeated the best that the world had to offer."

Genghis Khan's death in 1227 did nothing to slow the Mongol advance, as his son Ögedei continued the westward surge. By the year 1241, they had expanded their empire across Poland, Hungary, and parts of Germany. The European resistance consisted of local mercenaries, Teutonic Knights, and Knights Templar, who were quickly slaughtered. Western Europe had no answer to this unstoppable force from the East. Then the unexpected occurred.

In December of 1241, five thousand miles from the battlefield, Ögedei died suddenly, either from poisoning or the excesses of drink. Almost as quickly as they had appeared in Europe, the Mongols vanished. It was a custom among the Mongols that upon the death of the Great Khan, all armies were to be withdrawn to return home for the selection of a new Khan. They never returned.

ର   ର   ର

The Mongol army's failure to return to western Europe leaves open the intriguing question of what might have been had they continued their seemingly unstoppable march toward the Atlantic Ocean. In those areas of Asia and eastern Europe the Mongols had conquered, the physical destruction left behind was staggering. Whole villages were leveled, bridges were burned, and crops were destroyed. More important, entire populations were killed. The citizens who were spared—tradesmen and other skilled workers useful to the Mongolian nation—were either attached to the army or taken back to Mongolia. As a result, both the people with knowledge of how to rebuild the decimated areas and the manpower necessary to do so were absent, setting those parts of Asia and eastern Europe back centuries. The Mongol invasion was, in one view, "a major cause of the subsequent decline that set in throughout the heartland of the Arab East." By contrast, western Europe, left untouched, began an age of unparalleled technological advance. This included the adoption or invention of windmills, water mills, printing, gunpowder, the astrolabe, spectacles, scissors of the modern shape, better clocks, and greatly improved ships. Eventually this allowed the Europeans to venture farther into the surrounding world, starting their own conquest of foreign powers.

An even greater potential impact would have been the Mongols' ethnic and religious influence over the peoples that came under their control. In the conquered lands, the draconian penal laws set forth in the Yasa replaced the legal systems previously in place and a policy of religious tolerance weakened the role of Islam in government. Interestingly, however, the majority of the Mongol warriors ended up either converting to Islam or adopting many of its principles. As the armies spread farther west, the Mongols brought with them the Muslim religion, which became predominant in many of the lands they overran. Had they not abandoned their push through Europe due to the sudden death of their leader, we can only wonder if the Islamic religion would have replaced Christianity in all of mainland Europe.

Mongolian army helmet

5

1961 | Strangers on a Train

IN THE YEARS IMMEDIATELY FOLLOWING *the end of World War II, the London suburb of Dartford had a set of railroad tracks running through town that divided the more affluent homes from those situated in the more modest, some might even say poor, neighborhoods. K.R., the only child of a printer father and cake distributor mother, literally grew up on the "wrong side of the tracks," in what he later called a "foul housing project." Small in build, he was frequently the target of bullies and learned early on how to take a beating. Academics held little interest for him and his educational path eventually landed him in the local technical school, where he acquired a reputation as something of a rebel.*

K.R. took comfort in long walks with his grandfather, Gus, who played saxophone in a dance band in the 1930s and by the 1950s had moved on to the violin in a square-dance band. As a result, the walks the man and child took together often ended in one or more music shops. K.R. already had an interest in music—he was one of only three sopranos in the school choir until his voice began to change and he was kicked out—but Gus did little to directly push him farther. Instead, he slyly and without comment placed a guitar out on top of his piano before every visit, hoping to catch the boy's vivid imagination. Finally, when K.R. was around ten years old, Gus handed him the guitar and taught him a few basic chords. From then on, K.R. was self-taught by attempting to mimic what he heard on the radio or on the few records he was able to buy. He did not get a guitar of his own until he was fifteen.

Music did not tame the boy's rebellious nature, and he would be expelled from school thirty minutes before graduation for skipping a mandatory assembly. As a result, a sympathetic teacher arranged for him to attend Sidcup Art College, where he could study music in a relaxed atmosphere. He came to love American blues and to worship the music of Chuck Berry, whose records were difficult or impossible to find in England.

By contrast, M.J., who for a short time lived only a couple streets away from K.R. and who briefly attended the same school, was raised on the more privileged side of the tracks in the more genteel section of Dartford. Described as a normal, happy, and well-rounded child, as a young student he was at or near the top of his class in every subject and excelled at sports, perhaps the result of the influence of his father, a physical training instructor. A model student, with no signs of the rebellious nature of K.R., he easily passed the testing all eleven-year-olds were subjected to and moved on to a prestigious grammar school in Dartford. Suddenly placed among the area's best and brightest, he struggled in the sciences and was no longer among the best boys in sports.

M.J., too, found a refuge from the stresses of school in music. He was also a member of his school's choir, although his time there was undistinguished. He learned a bit of guitar on a simple instrument picked up as a souvenir on a family trip to Spain. Just like K.R., he discovered and nourished his love for "primitive music," as rock and roll was dismissively called at the time, by listening to late-night broadcasts of Radio Luxembourg. His first exposure to the music of Little Richard grabbed him, attending a concert by the penultimate showman Buddy Holly cemented his desire to explore new or unfamiliar forms of music, and once he discovered the blues he was hooked. He and three classmates formed a blues band, where M.J. shunned the guitar and chose instead to sing lead vocals and posture on stage.

M.J., like K.R., soon discovered that the music he wanted to hear was not available on records anywhere in the London area. He worked odd jobs to make enough money to order blues and rock records directly from the Chess Records headquarters in Chicago, including a summer stint at age 15 selling ice cream outside of the Dartford Town Hall, where he was once patronized by K.R. M.J. viewed the records he would receive from the States as a status symbol of sorts and was often seen carrying three or four of them under his arms.

In the fall of 1961, M.J. entered the London School of Economics, intending to become a teacher or civil servant. One foggy day in October of that year, he was on a train platform in Dartford waiting to catch the delayed 8:28 into London to attend an economics lecture. Dressed smartly in a beige wool cardigan and striped school scarf, he noticed a vaguely familiar face watching him. It had been years since they were schoolmates, but he and K.R. (deliberately dressing down in faded denim jeans and a lilac shirt) recognized and approached each other. The topic of conversation was a foregone conclusion, for under his arm M.J. held his usual stack of records; sitting on top, visible to K.R.'s eager eyes, was Chuck Berry's "Rockin at the Hops."

The two young men, aged 17 and 18, sat together on the train and discussed their musical idols, finding that they had nearly identical tastes in music. K.R. was so immersed in the conversation that he nearly missed his stop. After that first encounter, the two got together often, playing rock and blues records together and attempting to mimic the riffs they heard. Eventually they would sit in with blues bands playing local clubs. In 1962, along with three other English boys, they formed their own band and secured their first gig on July 12, 1962, at the Marquee Club in London. When one of their bandmates called the publication Jazz News to publicize their performance, he was asked the name of their band. It had come together so fast that no one had thought to come up with a name. Lying on the floor near the phone was a Muddy Waters record, one of the stack that M.J. had been holding on the train platform eight months before. The fifth track was "Rollin' Stone," and the band at that moment became the Rollin' Stones.

જી   જી   જી

Brian Jones was a member of the group at that first concert, and he, Keith Richards and Mick Jagger were soon joined by Bill Wyman and Charlie Watts to form the core group of what was soon renamed The Rolling Stones. Signed by Decca Records, the band went on to record nearly thirty studio albums, along with numerous live releases. Their first international number one hit, released in May of 1965, was "(I Can't Get No) Satisfaction." Since their formation in 1962, the band has sold over two hundred million records. They were inducted into the Rock & Roll Hall of Fame in 1989. Recently celebrating their fiftieth anniversary, the members of the group have changed throughout the years, but Keith Richards and Mick Jagger, who met by chance on the train platform as teenagers, remain.

Keith Richards and Mick Jagger in concert

6

Accidental Inventions

Internal Pacemaker

The first pacemaker, a device that helps the heart beat in a regular rhythm, appeared in 1899 when British scientist J.A. McWilliams discovered that electrical impulses could regulate the heartbeat at a steady sixty to seventy beats per minute. After that time, improvements were made to the devices, but they remained bulky units (some of them as large as an oven) that were used outside the body and required an external power source. While important in saving lives, pacemakers were awkward and expensive and hindered a person's ability to move around. They also tended to shock the patients using them.

In the mid-1950s, an electrical engineer teaching and working at the University of Buffalo named Wilson Greatbatch was researching improved methods to record heart sounds. While assembling one of his experimental contraptions, Greatbatch accidentally pulled the wrong transistor out of a box and inserted it into his machine. To his great surprise, instead of recording electrical pulses, it was actually producing them. In his words, "I stared at the thing in disbelief." Fortunately, he recognized the potential for what he had created, and spent the next two years working on making it small enough and effective enough to use inside the human body.

The first successful demonstration of the internal cardiac pacemaker took place on a dog in 1958. Shortly thereafter, it was implanted into a 77-year-old man, who lived for eighteen more months. Today, over a million people worldwide have internal pacemakers regulating their heartbeats.

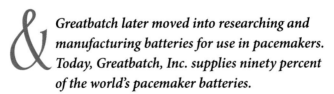

Greatbatch later moved into researching and manufacturing batteries for use in pacemakers. Today, Greatbatch, Inc. supplies ninety percent of the world's pacemaker batteries.

Brandy

Wine has been around for several millennia, but transporting it has always posed challenges. At one time it was stored in large, wooden casks and then loaded onto ships, where it could spend many months subject to changes in temperature and air pressure, which tended to alter its taste. In the early 1500s, an unknown Dutch trader attempted to address this problem. Since wine is mostly water, he distilled the liquid to remove most of the water, with the intent of adding the water back in when it reached its final destination in Holland. Doing so had the additional advantage of saving space (and therefore shipping costs) and reducing taxes, which were based on the volume of the wine.

Adding water back into the condensed substance the Dutch called "brandewijn" ("burned wine") met with mixed success. Importers found, however, that they liked the brandewijn better than the wine itself. Brandy has been a popular drink ever since.

> *Some people claim that drinking brandy in moderate amounts has several medical benefits, including heart health, anti-aging qualities, prevention of certain cancers, sleep inducement, boosting of the immune system, and help with respiratory issues.*

Brandy casks, early 1900s

POST-IT NOTES

Part of Spencer Silver's job with the 3M Company was to develop new adhesives that would improve on the strength and toughness of what the company currently had on the market. While experimenting in 1968, he produced an adhesive that was just the opposite—one that barely stuck at all and which could be easily removed and then reapplied. Silver was fascinated by his discovery, but didn't see any practical application and set it aside.

Years later, Silver mentioned his aberrant adhesive in a company seminar. In attendance that day was Art Fry, who had been experiencing problems losing his place in the hymnal while he sang in the church choir. The scraps of paper that Fry used to mark that day's hymns would invariably fall out. After the seminar he approached Silver about using his mystery substance to produce temporary bookmarks.

Over the next several years, Silver experimented with producing a commercially viable product that could be used as a bookmark. In the meantime, he provided all of 3M's employees with samples. The employees loved the removable sticky notes and found uses for them other than as simple bookmarks. At that point, Silver began to take the product much more seriously. Post-It Notes were introduced into a test market in 1977, then nationwide in 1980. They have been an office staple ever since.

1980 Post-It Note package

& *3M produces over 50 billion Post-It Notes each year. According to the company, the average professional receives eleven messages on Post-It Notes each day.*

VIAGRA

In the early 1990s, researchers at the American pharmaceutical company Pfizer, Inc. were attempting to create a drug that could expand a person's blood muscles and treat angina, a painful condition brought on when not enough blood is being pumped to the heart. During clinical trials for one promising drug, male subjects reported that they would get erections several days after taking it. At first, the Pfizer researchers chose to ignore that effect of the drug, as it seemed unlikely that there would be a market for a cure for erectile dysfunction that took days to work.

Eventually it became clear that the drug was ineffective in the treatment of angina. Around the same time, scientists began to publish studies that found that the inability to get or maintain an erection was not necessarily psychological, as was thought, but could be caused by a reduced blood flow to the penis. Pfizer switched gears and began serious research into whether the drug that failed to help with angina could assist men suffering from erectile dysfunction. The company patented Viagra in 1996 and it was approved by the FDA in 1998.

TEFLON

Hired by DuPont fresh out of Ohio State University in 1938, Roy J. Plunkett's first assignment was to research non-toxic chlorofluorocarbon refrigerants to use in refrigerators to keep them cold. Those used up to that time were not terribly efficient and tended to leak sulfur dioxide and ammonia, poisoning residents of the home. Plunkett produced a batch of a gas called TFE, distributed it among several cylinders, then froze the cylinders at extremely cold temperatures.

Later, when Plunkett and an assistant attempted to extract the gas, nothing would come out. Puzzled, they cut open a cylinder and discovered a white, powdery substance. Rather than dispose of it, Plunkett began to experiment to see if he could find any use for it. What he found was that it had a very high melting point, was non-corrosive, and extremely slippery (it was later designated as the third-slipperiest substance in existence).

Because it was expensive to produce, Teflon's first uses were limited to the industrial and military sectors, including use as an insulator for the Manhattan Project, the team of scientists that produced the first nuclear bomb. Since then, it has been instrumental in the production of computer chips, semiconductors, communication cables and architecture, and was even used to reduce friction between iron bars in the 1984 restoration of the Statue of Liberty.

The importance of Teflon was recognized early, and Plunkett received many awards for his discovery. At one early awards ceremony in 1951, DuPont sent all of the guests home with muffin tins coated with Teflon. These gifts proved popular, and in the 1960s DuPont introduced its popular line of non-stick baking pans.

Advertisement for first Teflon pan sold commercially

Plunkett's roommate at Ohio State, Paul Flory, won the Nobel Prize in chemistry in 1974.

Teflon is the only substance, natural or man-made, to which a gecko's feet cannot stick.

Ronald Reagan was called the "Teflon President" because criticism never seemed to stick to him.

SUPER GLUE

From one of the world's slipperiest substances to one of its stickiest: Super Glue. Its origin traces back to 1942, when Eastman Kodak employee Harry Coover was part of a team searching for materials that could be used to manufacture plastic gunsights for the military. By chance, he stumbled upon a formulation that literally stuck to everything. Focusing on the task at hand, and not seeing any use for the sticky substance, he set it aside and forgot about it.

The 1958 version of Super Glue

Years later, Coover was still at Eastman Kodak working as a supervisor for a project looking to develop a heat-resistant polymer for jet canopies. One of the researchers working under him, Fred Joiner, totally independent of Coover's earlier work, re-discovered the super-sticky substance (number 910 of the substances being tested) when he spread it between two prisms to test how well light could pass through it and then couldn't pry the prisms apart. Not only was the substance unsuitable for jet canopies, it created such a strong bond that Joiner realized he had just completely ruined an expensive piece of laboratory equipment. Unlike Coover, however, he immediately grasped its possible commercial applications. Seven years later, in 1958, it was released to the public under the catchy name "Eastman #910." Later the name was changed to the much more marketable "Super Glue."

Super Glue was used by medics during the Vietnam War to bind wounds together until a soldier could be transported to a field hospital.

One square inch of Super Glue can hold about one ton of weight.

7
1928 | The Moldy Dish

THE CIVIL WAR WAS BY *far the deadliest conflict in which America has participated in terms of American lives lost, with approximately 630,000 deaths. Of these, only about a third of the soldiers were actually killed in battle. The remainder died from infections and disease, primarily dysentery, but also pneumonia, tuberculosis, and other assorted illnesses. This trend continued even after the end of the war. In the late nineteenth and early twentieth centuries, bacterial infections were the leading cause of death among the U.S. population. According to the Centers for Disease Control and Prevention, diseases such as pneumonia, tuberculosis, diarrhea, and enteritis, along with diphtheria, caused a third of all deaths. Syphilis, gonorrhea, and meningitis were equally deadly. Contracting such an infection was often a death sentence; at that time, ninety percent of children who contracted bacterial meningitis died and the survivors were severely disabled. A simple ear infection, or even the common cold, could spread to the brain and on occasion be fatal.*

The statistics for World War I are no less grim. While it was the first war in history in which more soldiers died on the battlefield than from other causes, the spread of disease still killed millions of people, both military and civilian. In 1918, the final year of the war, twenty million people worldwide died in an influenza epidemic in which many deaths resulted from pneumonia or other bacterial infections. The medical profession had no answer.

One Scotsman coming back from the war, Dr. Alexander Fleming, decided to do something about it. A research assistant at St. Mary's Hospital in London, he saw first-hand how infection spread among the soldiers and could not be stopped. Upon his return he began to research staphylococci bacteria in the hope of discovering some way to stop its spread within the human body.

For many years, his efforts were unsuccessful. Then, after returning from vacation on September 28, 1928, he noticed that a mold called Penicillium notatum *had contaminated one of his petri dishes. Rather than toss it out, he put it under his microscope and to his surprise discovered that the mold had prevented the normal growth of staphylococci. The following year he published an article summarizing his findings in the* British Journal of Experimental Pathology, *to little reaction. Fleming continued to look for a practical application for his discovery, but was hampered by the hospital's limited resources, and in 1931 he moved on to other things.*

No one else immediately picked up where he left off, and his article didn't inspire other researchers to rush to apply his observations to the prevention of the spread of infection. It wasn't until 1938 that Howard Florey, professor of pathology at Oxford, was leafing through old issues of medical journals and found Fleming's article. Working with Ernst Chain, he began to develop a drug from the Penicillium notatum mold. The team's first test on a human occurred in 1940, when an Oxford police constable developed abscesses in his eyes, lungs, and shoulder after being scratched by a rose bush. For five days the officer was injected with the new drug and he began to improve. Unfortunately that exhausted the entire supply, and the man died.

The problem was in the production process. It took an astounding 528 gallons of mold culture to produce enough fluid for one dose of the drug and seven months to grow enough bacteria to cure a mere six patients. So in 1941 Florey and biochemist Norman Heatly flew to Peoria, Illinois, in search of a different strain of the penicillin mold that could make production more efficient. Again, chance played a role in advancing their efforts. One day a laboratory assistant brought in a cantaloupe covered in a golden mold, which was instantly seized upon by the researchers. This strain of penicillin yielded two hundred times as much of the drug, a figure increased to a thousand times more by enhancing it with X-rays and filtration. In March of 1942, they tried again on a dying patient. Anne Miller had developed an infection that led to blood poisoning, and she was near death. Happily, her name is now synonymous with the first person to be successfully treated with penicillin.

The world was at that time fully engaged in another world war, and no time was devoted to clinical trials of this new "miracle cure." Penicillin was rushed into the field and had an immediate and profound impact. Whereas in World War I the death rate from bacterial pneumonia was eighteen percent, in World War II it fell to less than one percent. By the end of the war, American companies were producing 650 billion units of the drug every month.

In 1965, Fleming, Florey, and Chain were awarded the Nobel Prize in Physiology and Medicine.

ભ   ભ   ભ

It is interesting to speculate when, if ever, penicillin would have been developed had Dr. Fleming thrown away his spoiled petri dish. Even after the publication of his paper in a medical journal in 1929, no significant efforts were made to develop a useable drug for almost a decade. A former assistant of Fleming, Cecil George Paine, had seen the famous dish and used a culture obtained from Fleming as part of a research project in his first job after leaving the lab. He used filtrates developed from the culture to treat eye infections in a coal miner and two infants and against

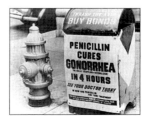

World War II government service announcement

all odds at the time saved the eyesight of all three, but he never published his results and did not pursue it further. No one else was even close to a breakthrough based on Fleming's findings until Florey took up the task.

It is impossible to calculate how many lives have been saved by penicillin, but near the end of the twentieth century some Swedish magazines (which called its development the most important discovery of the millennium) estimated the figure to be somewhere between one and two hundred million. Ironically, the overuse of antibiotics has led to certain bacteria developing resistance to their effects, creating the so-called "superbugs," and the future effectiveness of penicillin is unknown.

> "When I woke up just after dawn on September 28, 1928, I certainly didn't plan to revolutionize all medicine by discovering the world's first antibiotic, or bacteria killer. But I guess that was exactly what I did."
>
> ~Dr. Alexander Fleming

Laboratory flasks and test tubes used in development of penicillin, 1940

8

1915 | Missed the Boat

IN FEBRUARY OF 1895, CHICAGO *was the fastest-growing city in America, so little notice was taken when G. H. was born, the eighth and final child of a pair of Bohemian immigrants. As a youth he was slight of frame, and as a fourteen-year-old high school freshman weighed in at a mere 114 pounds. Despite his size, he played football and indoor baseball and ran track. Although baseball seemed to be the sport that suited G. H. best, his first love was football and he had a dream of playing the sport at the University of Illinois in Champaign-Urbana. For that reason, at the suggestion of his brother, he delayed enrolling in college immediately after high school in order to try to put on some weight.*

G. H. spent the year after high school working at the Hawthorn Western Electric Works in suburban Cicero. By the time he showed up to play football for the University of Illinois freshman team at age 19 the following fall, he tipped the scales at only 140 pounds. He made the team as a back-up halfback but saw little playing time that season. Determined to do better as a sophomore, G.H. returned to Western Electric to work during the summer after his freshman year.

The highlight of the year for any Western Electric employee was the company picnic, a fairly elaborate affair. Accustomed to working six days per week, the outing gave weary employees and their families the opportunity to have fun and relax. For the fifth annual event on July 24, 1915, this meant traveling from Cicero to Michigan City, Indiana, and to Washington Park, nestled along Lake Michigan and offering an amusement park with roller coasters and merry-go-round, picnic grounds, a beach, a bowling alley, and a pavilion for dancing. For G.H., it also meant playing a baseball double-header.

Tickets to the picnic cost 75 cents, and about seven thousand were sold. To transport the employees to the picnic grounds, Western Electric rented five excursion boats to sail the lake to Michigan City. The first boat, scheduled to leave at 7:30 a.m., was the S.S. Eastland, nick-named the "Speed Queen of the Great Lakes." G.H. planned to meet some friends at the dock to take the Eastland. *As he was leaving his home, however, his brother held him back for the purpose of weighing him, a delay which prevented G.H. from boarding the boat before it filled to capacity. (It should be noted that one of the friends he intended to meet, however, claims that G.H. simply overslept.)*

Without G. H., the Eastland *began to board at 6:30 a.m. and reached its capacity of 2,500 passengers by shortly after 7:00. Not long after it pulled away from the Clark Street Bridge, the ship began to roll and with little warning it capsized, trapping many of its passengers below deck. It happened so quickly that no life jackets had been handed out and no lifeboats were utilized. Despite the ship coming to rest in only twenty feet of water, and only nineteen feet from the wharf, 844 people died. The* Eastland *Disaster, as it came to be called, remains the worst inland maritime disaster in the country's history.*

ൈ   ൈ   ൈ

George Halas returned to the play football for the Illini that fall, but had a less than stellar career. As a junior, he broke his leg and was forced to stand on the sidelines for the entire season, which gave him the chance to observe legendary coach Bob Zuppke work his magic with the team, a lesson that would serve him well later. Even after enlisting in the Navy in 1917, Halas played football with the Great Lakes Naval Training Center team.

Following his discharge from the service, Halas's mother made him promise not to play football again and Halas at that time fully intended to keep his promise. He changed out one set of cleats for another and took the train south to Jacksonville, Florida, and the baseball training camp of the New York Yankees. He lasted until September of that first season but appeared in only twelve regular-season games for the 1919 team, batting an anemic .091 on two singles in twenty-one at bats, striking out eight times. Halas did not return to the Yankees in 1920. His inability to hit the curve ball was a blessing to generations of professional football fans.

Football remained in Halas's blood and, despite his promise to his mother, he joined up with a semi-pro team traveling the Midwest, earning about a hundred dollars per game. His educational background and playing career caught the attention of A.E. Staley, the owner of a corn products company in Decatur, Illinois, who felt that fielding a company team would be great publicity. Halas joined the company as employee, baseball player, and player-coach of the football team he was to create. His recruiting and coaching skills immediately brought success to the Decatur Staleys.

Earlier that year, five men had gathered inside a car dealership in Canton, Ohio, to form the American Professional Football Association. In its maiden season, teams had no set schedule, kept no records, and even had no set rosters, as players jumped from one team to another if it meant better pay. Many college players would play a game for their schools on Saturday and then earn money under assumed names playing professionally on Sunday.

The haphazard organization of the league threatened its existence, and after the 1920 season twelve independent team representatives again met in the dealership. Sitting on running boards and bumpers, eleven of the men listened as Halas talked. By the end of the meeting, each contributed $100.00 cash to join the league and the predecessor of the National Football League was formed.

That first season the Staleys played seven league games, all within a 125-mile radius of Decatur. The first—unofficial—championship, between the Staleys and the Akron Pros, ended in a 0-0 tie. In August of 1921 the league voted to allow the Green Bay Packers, coached by Curly Lambeau, to enter the league. The following January, with the Staley company facing financial difficulties, Halas moved the team to Chicago and reincorporated it as the Chicago Bears Football Club.

Tickets for games in the 1920 season ranged from fifty cents to a dollar. The face value of tickets to the 2016 Super Bowl started at $800.00, with a top price of $1,800.00. The highest price paid to a scalper for the 2017 Super Bowl was nearly $75,000.00 for a single ticket. Since the league was first formed, NFL teams have played more than fifteen thousand games.

Surviving passengers evacuate the *Eastland*

9

Duel #1
1704 | Button, Button...

THE CONCEPT OF TWO MEN *facing off with weapons in order to settle a dispute is nearly as old as humankind. In fact, duels were such an integral part of society that the first known laws regulating them were established in the early sixth century by King Gundebald of Burgundy, who declared that unresolved differences could be settled by means of trial by combat. Dueling emerged as a societal institution during the period of the Italian Renaissance, as easily offended aristocrats sought to improve their social standing by seeking vengeance for any perceived offense. Dozens of codes for the proper etiquette of dueling naturally followed and regulated everything from how to dress to rules of combat. The Royal Code of Honor of 1825, for example, forbade dueling on Sundays or near places of public worship, required the combating parties to salute each other before starting, and prohibited wearing any item of clothing that could distract the opponent, such as a military medal or ruffled shirt.*

The purpose of such rules was not to encourage dueling, just the opposite. Their intent was to make the process so cumbersome, and so full of loopholes, that the parties would find it easier to find satisfaction through negotiation. Unfortunately for some combatants, however, momentary passion led to the desire for immediate redress, and rules meant to give time for calmer heads to prevail were ignored. Such was the case for G.F.H.

G.F.H. was an 18-year-old musician when he arrived in Hamburg, Germany, to benefit from the tutelage of 23-year-old Johann Mattheson, an established tenor, harpsichordist, and conductor. Mattheson was doubtful of G.F.H.'s skill as a violinist, but recognized that he had talent at the keyboard. A tenuous bond was established between the two young men despite an undercurrent of jealousy that appears to have run both ways. Further strain was put on their relationship when Mattheson accepted a tutoring job that G.F.H. had thought would be offered to him.

The tensions came to a head during a performance of Mattheson's opera, The Misfortune of Cleopatra, *on December 5, 1704. As was customary at the time, Mattheson had dual roles in the production. On stage, he sang the part of Marc Antony. When he was not needed in that role, he proceeded to the orchestra pit, where he conducted the orchestra while also playing the harpsichord. In his absence, an opera composer named Reinhard Keiser was supposed to play the keyboard and lead the orchestra, but Keiser (who had a history of alcohol and gambling problems) left the production halfway through.*

After Marc Antony's death in Act III, Mattheson went to take Keiser's place at the harpsichord. To his surprise and annoyance, he found second violinist G.F.H. there instead, and G.F.H. refused to yield the position. Angry words soon followed, which quickly turned physical as the two men grappled and the fight spilled onto the street outside. Mattheson challenged G.F.H. to a duel while simultaneously pulling his sword and thrusting it into G.F.H.'s chest. His hit would certainly have been fatal, but the tip of his sword landed squarely on a large brass button of G.F.H.'s coat, breaking the tip. G.F.H.'s life was spared.

℮   ℮   ℮

It's unclear how the fight—or *The Misfortune of Cleopatra* for that matter—ended that night, but at some point the two men reconciled. Soon thereafter, however, George Frideric Handel left Hamburg and settled in Italy. His operas met with success there and drew the attention of the manager of the King's Theatre in London, where he was commissioned to write an opera. Within two weeks, the result was *Rinaldo*, the success of which catapulted Handel to fame. Today he is perhaps best known for his oratorio *Messiah* and its Hallelujah Chorus, which is especially popular at Christmastime.

The final bars of the "Hallelujah Chorus" from Handel's own score of *The Messiah*

10

1894 | Stale Wheat

THE PREVAILING ATTITUDE TOWARD SEX *in the Victorian era of the nineteenth century, at least in its public face, came about as a reaction to the perceived sinfulness of the sexual liberality of previous generations. Puritan morality and an official policy of sexual repression prevailed. "Scientific" studies claimed that sexual release, especially among males, led to feebleness, mental diminishment, and the impairment of artistic creativity. Men were counseled to conserve their mental health by avoiding fornication altogether. Male weakness in this regard would supposedly be passed on to the women and children, thus adversely affecting the mental acuity of the entire society.*

If having sexual relations with a partner was frowned upon, masturbation (more commonly referred to during that period as "onanism") was seen as an entirely new level of evil, with comparable consequences. Sickness and disability were frequently attributed to self-pleasuring, and certain sections of the scientific community (which seemed to spend an inordinate amount of time studying the subject) lectured that it was "beyond doubt" that masturbation led to insanity. Popular publications of the time included Onania: Or the Heinous Sin of Self-Pollution, and all its Frightful Consequences *and Samuel Tissot's* A Treatise on the Diseases Produced by Onanism. *Men, women, boys, and girls, both in Europe and in the United States, were inundated with supposedly indisputable evidence that sexual excitement, with or without a partner, was the primary cause of virtually every physical malady and social ill and should be avoided at all costs.*

Nowhere was there a more ardent proponent of the evils of sex than J.H.K., who hailed from a small town in the American Midwest. Born to Seventh-day Adventist parents—who shunned education for their children because they were convinced that the Second Coming was imminent and so schooling was unnecessary—Dr. J.H.K. nevertheless obtained a medical degree and went on to become the president and chief physician of the Battle Creek Sanitarium in Michigan. He, too, felt that sex of any sort was not only a moral failing, but led to physical and mental ailments requiring medical intervention (it is generally thought that J.H.K. never consummated his marriage for this reason). Masturbation, however, was far worse. J.H.K. once published a treatise cataloging thirty-nine different symptoms of a person plagued by this malady, including general infirmity, defective development, fickleness, both bashfulness and boldness, bad posture, stiff joints, acne, and epilepsy. In his words, "Neither plague, nor war, nor smallpox have produced results so disastrous to humanity as the pernicious habit of onanism."

29

One of the primary triggers leading to self-pleasuring, J.H.K. preached, was diet. He felt strongly that one should avoid all meat, alcohol, coffee or tea, condiments, and spicy foods, and only minimally consume eggs and dairy. "A man that lives on pork, fine-flour bread, rich pies and cakes, and condiments, drinks tea and coffee, and uses tobacco," he once said, "might as well try to fly as to be chaste in thought." As head of the sanitarium, he put his ideas into practice and subjected his unfortunate patients to as bland a diet as he could produce. Along with his brother, W.K., the facility's bookkeeper, he created a health treat he called "granula" (later changed to "granola"), a mixture of oatmeal and cornmeal baked into biscuits and then ground.

Along the same line, the brothers attempted to create an easily digestible form of bread by running boiled wheat flakes through a set of rollers. Their goal was to produce a dry, crisp food to stimulate saliva for healthy digestion in a form totally bereft of sexually exciting flavors. Over and over, their efforts failed and produced a sticky, gummy substance. One day, in the midst of another such experiment, the brothers were called away. When they returned, the wheat cake they were using had become stale and, in their view, useless. Rather than waste it, however, they ran it through the rollers anyway and found it produced a thin flake, which they then baked. In this way, Corn Flakes were born.

ભ   ભ   ભ

Soon, brothers John Harvey Kellogg and Will Kellogg agreed to share their discovery beyond the sanitarium's population, and in 1895 jointly formed the Sanitas Food Company. At the time, a ten-ounce box of cereal cost fifteen cents. Will was less focused on the anti-masturbatory goals of his brother and more on running a successful business, and in time pleaded with John Harvey to add sugar to the flakes to make them more appealing to the public. To John, this was heresy and the issue drove a wedge between the two men. In 1906, Will split from his brother and formed the Battle Creek Toasted Corn Flake Company. Corn Flakes became the first of many cereals to flood the market, eventually becoming the breakfast of choice. As of 2015, 2.7 billion boxes were being sold annually. Will's decision to add sugar also caught on: the cereal industry that same year used 816 million pounds of it.

Ironically, one of Dr. Kellogg's patients at the sanitarium was Charles William Post, who would go on to form one of Kellogg's chief rivals in the cereal business. Post said that his flakes were inspired by the cereal he ate while there; Kellogg claimed that he stole the recipe from an office safe.

Advertisement for Corn Flakes from around 1920

11

Late Thirteenth Century | The Winds of War

W E'VE ALREADY NOTED HOW THE *Mongol invasion of western Europe came to a complete halt with the unexpected death of their leader Ögedei in 1241. Undaunted, the Mongols turned their attention eastward later in the same century. Again, circumstances beyond their control intervened and prevented further conquest. This time, it was Mother Nature.*

Kublai Khan, the grandson of Genghis, was known more for his achievements in stabilizing the structure of his government than for his military conquests. Nevertheless, he enjoyed great success in using his armies to expand the Mongol empire and to unify the various dynasties of China. By 1268 A.D., his focus turned to one of the final holdouts, the Sung dynasty of Southern China. Unable to effectively use his cavalry to attack, due in part to the lack of forage for the horses in that part of the country, Kublai was forced to learn to build warships, which he then manned with experienced naval men from among the Chinese defectors. By 1276, they were able to occupy the Sung capital, and completed the defeat of their final formidable enemy within China when the last Sung emperor drowned in battle in 1279.

As he neared the victory that would cement his claim as the sole emperor of China, Kublai looked farther east to demand homage from neighboring Japan in 1274. Japan refused. Enraged, Kublai diverted 500 to 900 of his seagoing vessels carrying thirty to forty thousand men to force the issue with the Japanese. Anchored in Hakata Bay off of Kyushu, the Mongol forces were poised to attack the outnumbered Japanese forces. Just as the attack was about to be launched, a monstrous typhoon hit the coastline. A third of the Mongol ships were sunk, others were damaged, and thirteen thousand warriors drowned. The remainder of the battered fleet returned to China, too weakened to follow through on the attack.

Two years later, in 1276, Kublai reiterated his demand for homage from Japan. Again, he was refused. This time, his angry response was delayed while he completed his victory over the Sungs. Fresh off that triumph, he assembled what up to that time may have been the largest naval armada of the day. Two separate forces, one of forty-five thousand seasoned Mongol fighters and the other of 120,000 Sino-Koreans, boarded 4,400 warships and again sailed off to take by force what Japan would not give voluntarily.

It retrospect, perhaps the war party should not have assembled in the same harbor where it had met with disaster seven years earlier, but what were the odds of a second typhoon interfering with their plans? Apparently pretty good. Again, just as the armies were ready to assault a much smaller Japanese defense (by some counts, around forty thousand samurai and other fighters), a typhoon (later called a "kamikaze," or "divine wind" by the Japanese) hit with tremendous force. The damage this time was so great that only a few hundred of the invading ships survived and half of the Mongol warriors perished in the sea. Kublai did not try a third time.

☙   ☙   ☙

Some historians have doubted the veracity of these stories of Japanese good fortune, dubbing them unverified legends or tales invented to promote the idea that the people of Japan were favored by the gods and under their protection. In support of this argument, they point out that typhoons of such force are rare today, and that it would be extremely unlikely that there would be two within such a short time frame. Using modern science to investigate, University of Massachusetts Amherst geologist Jon Woodruff traveled to western Japan to analyze soil samples excavated from sediments beneath the lake bottom near the coast, close to where the Mongol forces were supposed to have readied their attack. He concluded that typhoons were more common in the area many centuries ago than they are today, and in fact sediment layers that dated to the late thirteenth century suggested two typhoons only a few years apart.

Typhoons, hurricanes, and cyclones are actually different names for the same weather phenomenon, the only difference being the location of the event. If the event is in the Atlantic or Northeast Pacific areas, it is a hurricane. In the South Pacific or Indian Ocean, it is called a cyclone. Typhoons occur in the Northwest Pacific.

Typhoon Lionrock makes landfall in northeast Japan in 2016

12

Accidental Inventions | Food Edition

CHOCOLATE CHIP COOKIES

After graduating from Framingham State Normal School Department of Household Arts in 1924, Ruth Graves Wakefield found work as a dietitian and food lecturer until 1930, when she and her husband purchased the Toll House Inn in Whitman, Massachusetts. As an innkeeper, she cooked all the meals for her guests, and in doing so established a reputation as being especially skilled in desserts. One day while in the middle of making an old colonial recipe for Chocolate Butter Drop Do Cookies, Wakefield discovered that she had run out of the baking chocolate that would melt as the cookies baked, spreading throughout the cookie. In desperation, she broke up a chocolate bar that she had received as a gift from Andrew Nestlé of the Nestlé Chocolate Company and dropped the pieces into the dough, expecting it to melt as it baked. Instead, the pieces survived the heat, and the Toll House "Chocolate Crunch Cookie" was born.

Nestle Toll House cookie tin, circa 1939

The cookie was an instant hit at the inn, but did not take off in popularity nationally until she printed the recipe in her cookbook "Tried and True" in 1938 and it was featured on the Betty Crocker Cooking School of the Air on the radio. Nestlé got Ruth's permission to print the recipe on the packages of their baking bars (reportedly in return for providing Wakefield a lifetime supply of chocolate), and continued to do so when the company introduced chocolate chips into the retail market in 1939. Nestlé's chocolate chips were marketed as "Toll House Chocolate Morsels" and the cookies became known as Toll House Cookies. The recipe, slightly altered, continues to be printed on every package of Nestlé Chocolate Chips.

    Americans consume around seven billion chocolate chip cookies each year. They are the official state cookie of both Massachusetts and Pennsylvania.

POTATO CHIPS

In the mid-1800s, one way New Yorkers chose to escape the heat of the summer was to head upstate to partake of the healing powers thought to be found in the mineral springs in Saratoga Springs, just north of Albany. One restaurant in the area, Moon's Lake House, was well known for its house specialty, Moon's Fried Potatoes. The potatoes were sliced thick, the traditional French method for serving them. Too thick, according to one disgruntled customer dining at Moon's in 1853. The unhappy man (legend has it that it was larger-than-life railroad and shipping magnate Cornelius Vanderbilt, although there is no proof of this) found the potatoes too thick and soggy for his taste and sent them back to the kitchen. He was just as unsatisfied with a second, thinner-cut portion, which he also returned.

George Crum

The cook that day was Native American George Crum, a temperamental former mountain guide and trapper. Outraged after seeing his treasured potatoes come back to the kitchen a second time, Crum wanted to teach the customer a lesson and sliced the potatoes extra-thin before frying them and dousing them with salt, knowing they would be too thin and crispy to be eaten with a fork. To his surprise, the customer raved about the creation. "Saratoga Chips" instantly became a staple on the menu.

Seven years later, Crum opened his own restaurant focusing on fish and game, where a basket of Saratoga Chips was placed on every table. His clientèle grew to include wealthy New Yorkers, including the Vanderbilts.

Crum never took steps to protect his creation, and in fact there is some doubt about whether he was the first person to make potato chips. His sister (or possibly sister-in-law) Catherine Speck Wicks, who also worked in the Moon Lake House kitchen, claimed that she accidentally dropped slices of potatoes she was peeling into a pan of fat that was heating in preparation for a batch of doughnuts.

Moon's Lake House, 1896

 Today, potato chips are America's favorite snack food; the average American eats four pounds of them each year.

SACCHARIN

Saccharin, so common today in the bright pink packets of Sweet'N Low found on restaurant tables, lays claim to being the first artificial sweetener and was created entirely by accident. Its roots trace back to 1877, when a Russian chemist named Constantin Fahlberg was hired by a company in Baltimore, Maryland, to analyze sugar shipments that the U.S. government had impounded over questions of purity. The same company also retained Ira Remsen, a professor of chemistry at (and later president of) nearby Johns Hopkins University, primarily to gain access to his laboratory. After the evaluation of the sugar was complete, Remsen allowed Fahlberg to stay on in the lab to conduct unrelated research involving the development of coal tar derivatives.

No-Cal Ginger Ale was introduced in 1952 as the first soda marketed to dieters. It did not use saccharin.

The fateful day began like every other, with Fahlberg experimenting with various combinations of chemicals. One such mixture of acid, phosphorus, and ammonia boiled over and got onto Fahlberg's hands. Fahlberg was apparently not one to concern himself with thoroughly cleaning up when his work was done for the day, as that night at dinner while eating a roll he noted the extraordinary sweetness of the crust. Realizing that the sweet taste was not coming from the roll but from a residue on his hands, Fahlberg rushed back to the lab and proceeded to taste every mixture he had created earlier that day. Upon reaching the combination that had boiled over, he knew he had stumbled upon a major find, a sweet success, if you will.

Fahlberg patented his invention in 1886 (ignoring any contributions of Remsen, who remained furious for the rest of his life), although saccharin did not become popular until World War I, when sugar was in short supply and the government looked for alternatives.

Saccharin (technically "anhydroorthosulphamine-benzoic acid") is 300 times as sweet as sugar.

Sucrolose, the active ingredient in Splenda, was also discovered by accident when a chemist working on developing an insecticide was told to test the powder, but misheard and thought he was supposed to taste it.

Popsicle® Pops

It seems appropriate that Popsicle® Pops were invented by an 11-year-old boy. It was a warm evening near San Francisco in 1905 when Frank Epperson mixed some powdered soda and water in a cup, stirring it with a stick. Apparently distracted, he forgot about his drink and left it outside on his porch overnight. Temperatures dipped and the mixture froze. The next day upon finding the cup, Frank pulled the drink out by the stick, tasted it, and became the first child to discover the wonders of the Popsicle®.

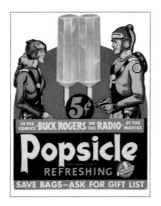 

Early Popsicle® advertisements

As a boy, Frank sold the occasional frozen concoction around his neighborhood, but it didn't start getting popular until he was a young man peddling "Epsicles" at Neptune Beach, a local amusement park similar to Coney Island, featuring roller coasters and a swimming pool. His children, though, called them "Pop's sicles," and that is the name that came to be associated with the treat through the years. In 1925, Epperson sold the rights to his creation to the Joe Lowe Co., which produced and sold Popsicle® Pops until 1989, when the company was sold.

 Today, over two billion Popsicle® Pops are sold each year. Cherry is the number one flavor.

Ice Cream Cones

As with most histories of popular food items, there are many competing claims to the origins of the ice cream cone. There is little question that Italian immigrant Italo Marchiony produced wafer-like cones with a frozen concoction inside commercially in 1896, and attempted to patent them in 1903. Even earlier, an etching of the Parisian Café Frascati in 1807 appears to show an image of what could be an ice cream cone. Nevertheless, it is conceivable that word of these (and other) efforts had not made it to

St. Louis, Missouri by 1904, and the legend of how ice cream cones were first invented is too good not to repeat.

The 1904 Louisiana Purchase Exposition, informally known as the St. Louis World's Fair, supposedly saw the debut of many iconic food items (most, it seems, created accidentally), including the hamburger, hot dog, peanut butter, club sandwich, cotton candy, and iced tea. Most of these, though, actually existed prior to the fair but gained wide exposure there. Add to this list the ice cream cone, which as noted also had origins elsewhere, but which apparently was accidentally created there through a fortuitous set of circumstances.

An area of over two acres was devoted to food items of every conceivable type, and some concession booths sold what at the time were considered unusual dishes. Syrian concessionaire Ernst A. Hamwi, for example, sold *zalabia*, a thin, crisp, pastry. When the ice cream vendor at the booth adjacent to him ran out of dishes, Hamwi rolled a *zalabia* into a cone shape and his neighbor filled it with ice cream. In the heat of a St. Louis summer, ice cream cones became an instant hit.

> *More ice cream is sold on Sunday than on any other day. It takes about 50 licks to eat a single scoop (yes, people do research these things).*

Philibert-Louis Debucourt's 1806 etching of the Café Frascati in Paris.
Note the woman seated at the table in the lower right-hand corner,
where she appears to be enjoying an ice cream cone.

13

1844 | - .... . / - . .-.. . --. .-. .- .--. ....

L ONG-DISTANCE COMMUNICATION WAS A problem for civilizations for thousands of years. Ancient civilizations devised codes in order to send messages by smoke signals or drumbeats, but such methods required a line of sight, generally situated on a high hill or plateau, and a series of relay stations. Rain, snow or wind could cause problems with visibility and could shorten the distance sound would travel. Later, semaphores, a series of large movable arms or flags, suffered from the same limitations.

Into this world came Samuel Morse, who grew up wanting to pursue a career as a painter and, against his father's wishes, as a young man sailed to England to study art. While there he achieved modest success portraying heroic historical figures and epic events in a broad, romantic style using vibrant colors. In 1815 he returned to the United States and set up a studio in Boston, Massachusetts, where he married Lucretia Walker.

Demand for his work was slow, so to make ends meet he began to travel around the East looking for commissions, which required spending a great deal of time away from home. He was working on one such commission in 1825 when he got word that his wife had grown gravely ill giving birth to their third child. Morse rushed home but was too late; his wife had died before he could get there.

In his grief, Morse was angry and frustrated that news of his wife's condition had taken so long to reach him that he was denied the opportunity to say goodbye. He continued to work, but after both of his parents died three years later Morse traveled to Europe to deal with his heartache. While in France he witnessed a demonstration on electromagnetism, which may have planted an idea in his head. On his subsequent voyage home, he met a fellow passenger named Charles Thomas Jackson, a geologist with a shared interest in the possibilities of electricity. To pass the time they discussed how electrical impulses might travel long distances over a wire. Around this time, a British team developed a form of telegraph signal using five magnetic needles that were moved by an electric current to point to a series of letters and numbers.

Morse returned to from Europe to his position teaching art at New York City University, but did not forget what he had learned on his trip. Motivated by the circumstances of his wife's death and buoyed by his chance meeting with Jackson, in his spare time, despite his complete lack of training in the field of electricity, he conducted experiments with magnets and wires. Eventually collaborating with Alfred Vail and Leonard Gale, he developed a simple system in which an operator pushed down a key to complete an electric circuit, which sent a signal to a receiver on the other end of the wire. All the system needed to work was a wire, a key, a battery and a line of poles to carry the wire between stations.

Initially, their invention elicited little excitement and, more important, no funding with which to pursue its potential. It took an actual act of Congress to finally move the telegraph forward, when the government agreed to supply the funds to set up a test wire running the forty miles between Washington, D.C., and Baltimore, Maryland. The test conducted on May 24, 1844, using the new system of dots and dashes invented by Morse and Vail, was a success and the telegraph system created out of one man's grief spread quickly around the world, transforming it forever.

> "What hath God wrought!"
> ~Test message sent from Morse to Vail,
> May 24, 1844

An early Morse telegraph key

14

Famous People Who Eluded Death

ARTURO TOSCANINI, ORCHESTRAL CONDUCTOR

Toscanini, an Italian conductor whose credits include leading the first public performance of Rossini's *La Boheme,* was scheduled to return to Europe aboard the luxury liner *Lusitania* but grew ill from the stress of overwork, cut his musical tour short, and instead left aboard an Italian ship a week earlier. The *Lusitania* was torpedoed by German submarines on May 7, 1915, and sank in only eighteen minutes. Almost twelve hundred passengers perished.

The *Lusitania* steaming into port, sometime around 1907-1913

JEROME KERN, BROADWAY COMPOSER

Kern was also supposed to travel on the *Lusitania,* but missed the boat when his alarm didn't go off and he overslept. He went on to compose the music for over seven hundred songs, including the score for *Show Boat,* and won two Academy Awards for Best Original Song.

Promotional photo of the original 1928 stage production of *Show Boat*

ADMIRAL RICHARD E. BYRD, EXPLORER

In August of 1921, Byrd was scheduled to join a crew on a trial flight of a new navy dirigible known as the ZR-2, but missed the train the day before, got to the airfield late and was scratched from the crew. The dirigible broke in half and exploded in midair, crashing into a river and killing forty-four American and British crew members. Eight years later, Byrd and his crew became the first people to reach the South Pole in a flight that took over eighteen hours.

U.S. Navy Lt. Com. Byrd in front of his Bluebird seaplane

CARY GRANT, ACTOR

Along with fellow actor George Murphy, Grant was scheduled to be on board the Pan Am Clipper "Yankee" in February 1943, but their itinerary was changed at the last minute. The plane crash-landed, killing twenty-four passengers and crew. Grant was one of the most popular actors of his time, appearing in seventy-six films (including four Alfred Hitchcock classics) and was awarded an honorary Oscar in 1970.

Cary Grant in a scene from 1939's *North by Northwest*

WAYLON JENNINGS, COUNTRY SINGER

Jennings was playing bass in Buddy Holly's backup band in 1959 on a tour plagued by an old tour bus that kept breaking down and had no heat. The bus's problems motivated Holly to charter a small plane for himself, his guitarist, and Jennings to fly from a gig in Clear Lake, Iowa, to their next concert in Minnesota. Jennings gave up his seat on the plane to J. P. Richardson (the Big Bopper), who was suffering from the flu. When Jennings told Holly he was taking the bus, Holly jokingly told him he hoped the bus broke down, and Jennings retorted, "I hope your ol' plane crashes." The plane did in fact crash, killing Holly, Richardson, and Ritchie Valens, an event immortalized in Don McLean's 1971 song "American Pie." Jennings was inducted into the Country Music Hall of Fame in 2001.

Jennings and Holly in a New York City photo booth in 1959

ELIZABETH TAYLOR, ACTOR

In 1958, Taylor was due to accompany her husband Mike Todd on a private plane (named the *Lucky Liz*) but she canceled due to a cold and 102-degree fever. The plane was overloaded while flying in icy conditions, causing engine failure. The crash killed Todd and the other three occupants of the plane. Taylor lived another fifty-three years and won two Oscars for Best Actress, including one for her performance opposite Richard Burton in *Who's Afraid of Virginia Woolf?*

Michael Todd and Elizabeth Taylor

MAARTEN DE JONGE, DUTCH CYCLIST

Riding for a cycling team based in Malaysia, de Jonge flies to competitions all over the world. On March 8, 2014, he was booked on Malaysia Airlines Flight 370, but changed flights to avoid a stopover in Beijing. The plane disappeared mid-flight and is still missing. On July 17 of that same year, he had a ticket on MA Flight 17 but switched at the last minute in order to take a cheaper flight. MA 17 was shot down over the Ukraine.

ଔ ଔ ଔ

On September 11, 2001, four airplanes flying domestically within the U.S. were hijacked by terrorists. American Airlines Flight 11 and United Airlines Flight 175 were forced to crash into the Twin Towers in New York City, American Airlines Flight 77 was steered into the Pentagon in Virginia, and United Airlines Flight 93 crashed into a field in Pennsylvania. Nearly three thousand people died in the attacks. Afterward, many stories emerged from people who survived by chance. Here are just a few:

PATTI AUSTIN, SINGER

Austin was booked on Flight 93 but had to change to a flight a day earlier after being notified that her mother had had a stroke. An award-winning singer, her 2008 album *Avant Gershwin* won the Grammy Award for Best Jazz Vocal.

IAN THORPE, ATHLETE

In his career, the Australian swimmer won five Olympic gold medals, still the most won by any of that nation's athletes. On September 11, he was in New York City jogging and planned to visit the observation deck of the World Trade Center to take pictures, but forgot his camera.

MARK WAHLBERG, ACTOR

Wahlberg was supposed to be on American Airlines Flight 11 but changed his plans at the last moment and canceled his ticket. Wahlberg appeared in the popular television series *Entourage* and has appeared in many movies, including *The Italian Job, Ted,* and *Transformers: Age of Extinction.*

SETH MCFARLANE, ANIMATOR AND VOICE ACTOR

An error by McFarlane's travel agent saved his life. He was scheduled on Flight 11, but the agent told him the flight left at 8:15 instead of its actual departure time of 7:45. He missed the flight, getting there just a few minutes after boarding ended.

MICHAEL LOMONACO, CHEF

As head chef of the restaurant Windows of the World, located on the 106th and 107th floors of the World Trade Center, Lomonaco was heading to his office when he made an impromptu decision not to wait for his noon appointment to get his glasses repaired, and stopped off at Lens Crafters at 8:15 a.m. instead. The thirty-minute delay in getting to work meant he was in the lobby of the World Trade Center when he heard an unusual rumble, and stepped outside to investigate.

SARAH FERGUSON, DUCHESS OF YORK

Ferguson was due to be in the offices of her charity "Chances for Children," which were on the 101st floor of 1 World Trade Center, but was running late due to an interview in the NBC studios.

Sarah Ferguson and Prince Andrew in their wedding coach

JOHN THOMPSON, COACH

Thompson, at the time the head basketball coach at Georgetown University, cancelled his plans to be on Flight 77 in order to appear on a talk show.

JULIA CHILD, CHEF

The legendary chef and her assistant were booked on Flight 11, but her producer insisted that she be filmed in her kitchen for the Smithsonian's Museum of Natural History on September 11, the only day the film crew had available. Child rescheduled her flight for later in the week.

Julia Child in public television's groundbreaking series *The French Chef*

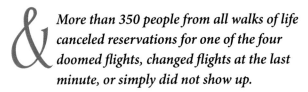

More than 350 people from all walks of life canceled reservations for one of the four doomed flights, changed flights at the last minute, or simply did not show up.

15

1862 | The Hazards of Smoking

IT HAD BEEN SEVENTEEN MONTHS *since the first shot of the Civil War was fired at Fort Sumter, and in the fall of 1862 the war was not going well for the North. The South's General Robert E. Lee had put together a string of victories in battle and the North was on the defensive in Maryland, Kentucky, and Tennessee. In Washington, D.C., politicians and ordinary citizens alike feared that the nearby rebels would soon invade the capital. Lee shrewdly decided to take advantage of these fears, as well as the South's momentum, by moving into Maryland and Pennsylvania. Although he knew that he could not take permanent control of the area, he felt that a decisive victory on Northern soil would so weaken the North's resolve to continue the carnage that they would be forced to sue for peace.*

Pursuant to this goal, on September 9, 1862, Lee issued Special Order 191 detailing his battle plans. It called for the Southern troops to continue their march toward Harper's Ferry as the immediate objective, but also divided three divisions off of the main force and further divided General Stonewall Jackson's command into three parts, the idea being that they would close in on Harper's Ferry from each of the three mountains overlooking it. As was customary, Lee himself did not transcribe the order. Several copies were handwritten on his behalf by Colonel Robert H. Chilton, his assistant adjutant-general, to be distributed to certain officers. One of the intended recipients of Special Order 191 was Major-General Daniel Harvey Hill. For reasons lost to history, two copies of the order were addressed to Hill. One of them ended up in his possession; the fate of the second one changed the course of the war.

On September 13, the XII Corps (Twelfth Army Corps) of the Army of the Potomac made camp near Frederick, Maryland, not far from an area once occupied by the rebel army. Tired and hot, Corporal Barton W. Mitchell of the 27th Indiana Infantry sought out the shade of a tree in a field of clover. His attention was soon drawn to a bulky envelope on the ground, which turned out to be three cigars wrapped in paper and tied with string. Elated, he sought out a friend to share the smokes. While unwrapping their treasure, the men's curiosity was drawn to the paper in which the cigars rested. Recognizing that it may be of some importance, they turned the document over to an officer who quickly passed it up the chain of command.

Hill's second copy of Special Order 191 was soon brought before General George B. McClellan, the commander of the Northern forces. Notoriously cautious, McClellan suspected a trap. As luck would have it, a colonel on the General's staff had known Robert Chilton before the war and recognized his handwriting. This was enough to convince even McClellan that the document was genuine, and he modified his battle strategy to respond to the division of Lee's troops.

No evidence exists to pinpoint how the order ended up wrapped around cigars in a field of clover. The best theory is that a courier wrapped the cigars in order to keep them dry from his own perspiration before placing them in his coat pocket. Stopping to rest under the same tree later sought out by Corporal Mitchell, he took off his coat and the cigars slipped out, a fact he did not notice until he had ridden on.

ભ   ભ   ભ

McClellan did not take immediate advantage of the information obtained from the Special Order, waiting eighteen hours before moving against Lee's divided army, a delay that allowed Lee to partially regroup. Many historians believe that had McClellan mobilized his troops the same morning that Lee's strategy was revealed to him, he could have destroyed the Army of Northern Virginia and possibly ended the war. Even so, the misplaced intelligence greatly benefited the Northern commanders, and the Battle of Antietam (also known as the Battle of Sharpsburg) was devastating for the South. Lee's army was badly hurt, the Confederacy never again was so close to victory, and the war's momentum switched to the North. Years later, Major Walter Taylor of Lee's staff wrote that "the loss of this battle order constitutes one of the pivots on which turned the event of the war." Historians agree.

Just as important as the lost battle was the change in perception of the war overseas. Prior to the Battle of Antietam, Jefferson Davis sent envoy James Mason to England with the goal of getting the British to recognize the Confederate government and to establish diplomatic ties. Doing so would have enabled the South to receive badly needed aid and could have meant Southern independence. The British, despite believing that the South was on the verge of victory, stalled. The Southern defeat at Sharpsburg killed any chance for recognition by England.

> " *The odds against the occurrence of such a chain of events must have been a million to one. Yet they happened.*
>
> ~Historian James M. McPherson

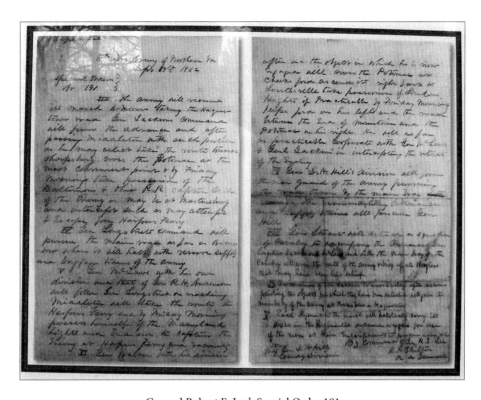

General Robert E. Lee's Special Order 191

16
Duel #2
1842 | Trench Warfare

WHILE SERVING AS A STATE *legislator in 1842, A.L. was a strong supporter of the State Bank of Illinois. It was a bitter pill to swallow, then, when the bank went bankrupt and was forced to close. Once it closed, its bank notes (essentially promissory notes of various denominations payable to the bearer, the equivalent of cash) became worthless. It naturally followed that James Shields, the State Auditor, announced that the state would no longer accept State Bank of Illinois' notes in payment of taxes. While that was a reasonable step, Illinois' Whig Party, including A.L., used Shields' position as a political tool to attack both him and his Democratic Party.*

Rather than vent his ire directly, A.L. used his friendship with the editor of the Sangamo Journal *to publish a series of satirical and critical letters under various pseudonyms, his favorite being that of a woman named "Rebecca." In one such letter published by the paper, "Aunt Becca" reported on her neighbor's supposed viewing of Shields' behavior at a local county fair, a portrayal that characterized Shields as a vain lout bragging of his attractiveness to women.*

Despite Shields's short temper, A.L.'s letters themselves were not enough to solicit anything more than a measured response. Unfortunately, A.L.'s fiancé Mary and her friend decided to get in on the fun and wrote their own letters, also under false names, which lacked the restraint or tact of those written by "Rebecca." The tone of their letters to the editor changed from satirical to insulting, and pushed Shields over the edge.

Shields confronted the Journal's editor, who gave up A.L.'s name. Shields immediately sent a written demand for satisfaction to A.L., who received it while at a courthouse. A.L. was a peaceable man and wanted to issue an apology to Shields, which most likely would have ended the conflict. A young doctor friend of A.L.'s, however, encouraged him to stand up like a man and refuse to apologize, which would trigger a duel. A.L. gave in to his so-called friend's prodding, and the duel was on.

As the challenged party, A.L. could choose the weapons and the rules of engagement. Hoping that setting ridiculous parameters for the duel would encourage Shields to change his mind, A.L. chose large cavalry broadswords as the weapons (Shields' reputation as an excellent shot with a pistol might also have been a factor in this decision). In addition, the men would be confined to a pit with a board running down the middle, with each combatant forced to remain on his side of the board. Unfortunately for A.L., even these unusual conditions did nothing to convince Shields to back down.

The two duelists and their seconds, then, had no choice but to arrange the duel. Moving across the Mississippi River to Missouri, as dueling was against the law in Illinois, the pit was dug and the men placed into it on their respective sides of the board. A.L. was a tall and lanky man, and while warming up used his sword to reach to the tree branches above Shields's side of the pit to cut them down. Shields, a mere 5'7" tall, immediately recognized how much strength it took to so easily cut the branches, as well as the advantage A.L. had in his reach. He quickly took his second's advice and called off the duel.

ଓ   ଓ   ଓ

Shields lived to see another day and later became a U.S. Senator. Abraham Lincoln, of course, became the sixteenth President of the United States. Shortly after the abortive duel, Lincoln stated that he only would have hurt Shields in self-defense, but in that event "could have split him from the crown of his head to the end of his backbone." The whole event was an embarrassment to Lincoln, however. He rarely spoke of it afterward and if the topic arose would quickly change the subject.

By Lincoln's time, the tradition of dueling had long crossed the ocean to the Americas. The first recorded duel occurred in the Massachusetts colony in 1621, only a year after the Pilgrims landed at Plymouth Rock. That conflict, fought with swords between Edward Doty and Edward Lester, resulted in no fatalities.

At first, Americans followed the European rules for dueling, including the "Code Duello" created by a group of Irishmen in 1777. That changed in 1838 when the former Governor of South Carolina, John Lyde Wilson, created an Americanized version. By mid-century, the American Code (or a version of it) contained twenty-five specific rules governing duels, including one that stated that "the parties engage until one is well blooded, disabled, or disarmed, or until, after receiving a wound, and blood being drawn, the aggressor begs pardon." While flintlocks were the preferred weapon of choice, they were notoriously inaccurate even in the hands of skilled marksmen. Accuracy was also made more difficult by a gentlemen's rule that it was dishonorable to take aim at an opponent for longer than a three-second period.

Contemporary etching of Lincoln showing off
his reach prior to his duel with Shields

17

Stars Discovered Purely By Chance

LANA TURNER, ACTOR

The discovery of blond bombshell Turner, one of the greatest sex symbols of the 1940s and 1950s, occurred in the most clichéd of ways. She was a student at Hollywood High School when the publisher of *The Hollywood Reporter* saw her drinking a soda in the Top Hat Café. He introduced her to Zeppo Marx of the Marx Brothers, who helped get her a small role in the unmemorable movie, *They Won't Forget.* Her tight skirt and sweater made an impression on moviegoers, however, and earned her both more film roles and the nickname, "Sweater Girl."

JOHN WAYNE, ACTOR

Marion Robert Morrison's aspirations to become a professional football player ended, along with his athletic scholarship at the University of Southern California, when he injured himself body surfing. To make ends meet, he took a job at Fox Films moving furniture and equipment, handling props, and doing any other sort of grunt work that he was asked to do. His strong build didn't go unnoticed and he was occasionally asked to work as a stand-in. This led to small roles in films by legendary director John Ford and eventual stardom.

Movie poster featuring Lana Turner and John Wayne (1955)

MARILYN MONROE, ACTOR

Born Norma Jeane Mortenson, Monroe spent a childhood in various orphanages before landing a job at a munitions plant inspecting parachutes and spraying airplanes with fire retardant. A photographer at the plant shooting a promotional piece for *Yank* magazine put her on the cover and recommended that, with her looks, she should consider acting. She took the advice to heart, started taking acting lessons, and a legend was born.

Marilyn Monroe posing for photographers during the filming of *The Seven Year Itch* in 1954

PAMELA ANDERSON, ACTOR

Anderson was only a face in the crowd at a British Columbia Lions football game in her native Canada until a cameraman noticed she was wearing a Labatt's shirt and featured her on the Jumbotron. The crowd's overwhelming reaction led management to bring her onto the field. Her first role was as a recurring character in the soap opera *Days of Our Lives* in 1992.

ASHTON KUTCHER, ACTOR

Kutcher was studying engineering at the University of Iowa when he was approached randomly in a local bar by a talent agent, who encouraged him to enter a modeling competition. Kutcher entered on a whim and ended up winning it, which led him to enter other competitions. His success brought him to the attention of advertising agencies representing Versace and Calvin Klein. Like many models, he later made the jump to acting.

JOHNNY DEPP, ACTOR

Depp dropped out of school when he was fifteen to pursue a career in music and played in some mildly successful bands. Hoping to build on that, he moved out to Los Angeles. While there he drove a friend to an audition for a part in Wes Craven's *A Nightmare on Elm Street*. Craven asked Depp to audition as well and (helped by Craven's teenage daughter, who thought Depp was "dreamy" and insisted that he be in the film) his acting career was off and running.

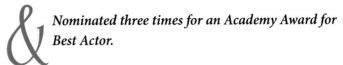

Nominated three times for an Academy Award for Best Actor.

CHARLIZE THERON, ACTOR

Theron was studying ballet in her native South Africa before a knee injury put an end to that career. She modeled a bit in the U.S. until 1994, when her mother bought her a one-way ticket to Los Angeles. Since she lacked any acting experience, no agent would take a chance on her. Frustrated and broke, Theron was given a small lifeline when her mother sent her a $500.00 check for expenses. When her bank refused to cash the out-of-state check, Theron threw a huge fit, verbally eviscerating the unfortunate bank teller, a performance that attracted the attention not only of the bank's other customers but of an agent waiting in line behind her. He landed her a three-second non-speaking role, but it started a huge career.

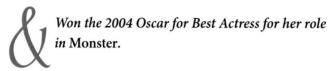

Won the 2004 Oscar for Best Actress for her role in Monster.

JASON STATHAM, ACTOR

Statham's acting career was going nowhere, so he resorted to doing anything he could just to eat, including selling counterfeit perfume and jewelry on the streets of London. This led to work as a model for French Connection, where he was introduced to director Guy Ritchie, who was intrigued by his illicit street sales and asked that Statham persuade him to buy a piece of fake jewelry. Statham's pitch convinced Ritchie to cast him as the streetwise con artist in his current production, *The Italian Job.*

JENNIFER LAWRENCE, ACTOR

Unlike many children, Lawrence did not grow up dreaming of being the next Hollywood star. While on a trip into Manhattan at the age of fourteen, she was approached by a talent scout who swore that he could get the girl into modeling. Surprisingly trusting, her mother allowed the man to take her daughter's picture and gave him her phone number. Agencies started calling and Lawrence agreed to go to a few shoots out of boredom. She quickly realized it wasn't the career path for her and moved into acting.

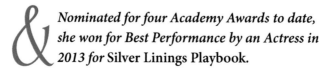

Nominated for four Academy Awards to date, she won for Best Performance by an Actress in 2013 for Silver Linings Playbook.

TONI BRAXTON, SINGER

Braxton began singing in church choirs as a young girl, although her strict parents limited her repertoire solely to gospel songs. She and her sister would watch *Soul Train* when their parents were away, however, so she did have limited exposure to secular music. The Braxton sisters had some success at local talent shows, but at that time went no further. Braxton went to college to become a music teacher, a path that was changed forever when songwriter Bill Pettaway overheard her singing to herself while she was pumping gas into her car. He helped the sisters sign with Arista Records in 1990, and while they found no success as a group, their single garnered the attention of producers who signed Braxton individually as the first act on their new label.

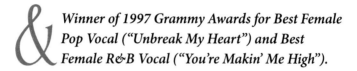

Winner of 1997 Grammy Awards for Best Female Pop Vocal ("Unbreak My Heart") and Best Female R&B Vocal ("You're Makin' Me High").

ROSARIO DAWSON, ACTOR

Dawson was fifteen years old and simply sitting on the front porch of her home enjoying a beautiful day when a Hollywood screenwriter and photographer, who were scouting locations in the neighborhood, walked by. They approached her and suggested that she would be perfect for a role in the writer's most recent screenplay. Despite having no prior acting experience other than one episode of *Sesame Street* as a child, she auditioned and was awarded the role of Ruby in the 1995 film *Kids*.

NATALIE PORTMAN, ACTOR

Eleven-year-old Portman was eating pizza with her family in Long Island, her face covered with marinara sauce, when a Revlon representative approached their table and convinced her parents to allow her to pursue modeling. She did, and had a very successful career doing so before turning her talents to acting.

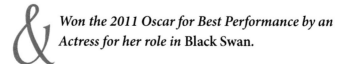

Won the 2011 Oscar for Best Performance by an Actress for her role in **Black Swan.**

18

312 A.D. | A Sign from Heaven

WE'VE ALREADY SEEN HOW JAPAN *was saved from disaster by a pair of timely storms, but some historians believe that Christianity would have perished were it not for another natural phenomenon, the appearance of a comet over a battlefield.*

In the centuries following the death of Christ, his followers had to endure persecution from a series of Roman emperors. In the middle of the third century, when about one million people professed to be Christian, Decius sought to stabilize his empire and create unity among his Roman subjects by commanding all Christians to deny their faith and to participate in the pagan worship favored by the ruling party. To help convince the citizenry that refusing was not an option, Decius had the Pope executed and instructed his soldiers to kill any Christians who would not obey the royal edict.

Despite the forceful and fatal hand of the Roman rulers, Christianity survived and grew, and by the turn of the century counted around six million faithful. The growth of the Christian religion corresponded with a weakening of the Roman empire, and the unfortunate Christians were blamed for this precipitous decline. Diocletian, one of the Roman emperors (there were at that time several that served simultaneously) became so intolerant of Christians that he banned the religion altogether and ordered Christians to relinquish all scripture. Any believers who refused were burned alive with their books. Throughout the first decade of the fourth century, followers of Jesus were subject to a more persistent and cruel persecution than at any time before.

During this period of religious oppression, a young military leader named Constantine served at Diocletian's side, expecting to follow his father Constantius Chlorus as an emperor of Rome. Diocletian instead anointed Constantine's rival (and son of Constantius's predecessor) Maxentius as his successor, after which Constantine returned to his father. Constantius died in 306 and Constantine claimed his title as an Augustus, a move that did not sit well in Rome, where Maxentius was favored. In 308, a conference was called to sort out the situation. To Constantine's dismay, Maxentius and his father-in-law were named "senior" emperors, while Constantine was relegated to junior status.

Other men also claimed the status of emperor; in fact, in 310 no fewer than five Romans called themselves by that title. Maxentius used his power in part to continue to suppress the Christian faith and to revive and support pagan beliefs and rituals. Perhaps in defiance of all that Maxentius stood for, or to distinguish himself from his chief rival,

Constantine courted Christians and may have at that time shared their faith. Certainly, he used it to further his own ambitions, as he "fused the viguor of the Christian faith with the power of the army." In any case, the seed may have been planted.

Tensions continued to build, and the rift between Maxentius, who had the support of Rome, and Constantine, who had built a following outside of the city, grew to the point where a final confrontation was inevitable. The fateful day came in the year 312, as Constantine's army overran Italy and reached the Milvian Bridge over the Tiber River, a few miles from Rome. Maxentius' forces massed on the other side of the river. Each knew that the decisive moment was at hand and that only one leader would emerge as a true emperor of Rome.

As the battle loomed, Constantine may have had anxiety as to the outcome. He was badly outnumbered; his forty thousand soldiers faced an army three times that size. About noon, as both sides readied their attacks, Constantine glanced to the sky and saw what he called a "cross of light" streaking across the heavens. Believing that the meteor was a sign, he found the courage to overcome his doubts and led his army to a decisive victory.

As a result of the battle, Constantine became the most powerful man in all of the Roman empire. His support of the Christian religion, and his own conversion, opened a new era for the church. He ordered an end to persecution and enacted a policy of tolerance toward all faiths. Christianity flourished. By the middle of the century, thirty-four million people professed to be Christian. Constantine credited divine intervention, represented in the form of a streaking comet, for his victory and the subsequent spread of the Christian faith.

ଓ ଓ ଓ

In 1999, a young Swedish scientist named Jens Ormo traveled to study at the International School of Planetary Studies near the Adriatic coast of Italy. Consulting a guidebook in anticipation of hiking in the nearby mountains, he came across a picture of a lake that he was convinced was formed as a result of a crater formed by the impact of an asteroid falling to Earth.

An expedition confirmed that the lake actually was a crater, and carbon dating estimated that it was formed in the late fourth to early fifth century. Is it possible that it fell a bit earlier, around the time of Constantine's battle? The fireball from the asteroid would have only lasted about ten seconds, but would have been brighter than the sun even in daytime. In addition, the force of the impact would have released energy fifteen times greater than the atomic bomb dropped on Hiroshima. If it had landed anywhere near Maxentius's army, it could have helped overcome the disparity in the size of the armies.

Bust of Constantine, Capitoline Museums, Rome

19

1970 | Bringing Down the (White) House

BOB WOODWARD WAS NEARING THE *end of his five-year stint in the Navy when he was assigned to the Pentagon as a watch officer overseeing worldwide teletype communications for the chief of naval operations, Admiral Thomas H. Moorer. Although the position brought with it top secret security clearance, his duties were often mundane and boring. One such task was to deliver sealed envelopes to military personnel, which frequently entailed waiting for long periods of time for the proper person to sign for the packet. It was during one of these idle periods in early 1970 that Lieutenant Woodward found himself spending the evening sitting in a waiting room not far from the Situation Room and offices of the National Security Council in the lower level of the West Wing of the White House.*

Before long an officer with a commanding presence and air of authority entered the room and sat, apparently also waiting for someone. Woodward attempted to make conversation but the man appeared uninterested in talking. Undeterred and bored, Woodward began talking about himself and eventually elicited the information that the stoic man's name was Mark Felt and that he was the Assistant Director of the Federal Bureau of Investigation, third from the top after J. Edgar Hoover. Woodward, insecure about the direction he wanted to take upon leaving the Navy and eager for career advice from such a powerful and influential man, began talking non-stop about himself and peppering Felt with questions. For a long time Woodward's monologue had no effect, and he felt his "patter verged on the adolescent," but he eventually stumbled onto a topic for which the two men had common ground, and Felt engaged the young Lieutenant in an extemporaneous career-counseling session. The men soon parted, with Felt giving Woodward his phone number at the FBI, neither suspecting that their chance meeting would set the stage for the resignation of a President.

Woodward kept in touch with Felt, continuing to ask his advice about possible careers. Against Felt's advice, and despite having no experience in journalism, Woodward talked the Washington Post *into giving him a two-week tryout as a reporter for the newspaper. It went disastrously, and Woodward was let go. Undeterred, he took a job at a small weekly paper, before again being hired by the* Post *at a salary of $165 per week. He enthusiastically threw himself into the job, taking any assignment he could in order to gain experience and exposure. In the meantime, Felt was promoted to managing all of the day-to-day activities of the FBI. Woodward occasionally would use Felt as a source, which Felt agreed to so long as any information he supplied was never attributed to him or to the FBI.*

On June 17, 1972, the Post's news desk got word that five men carrying electronic eaves-dropping equipment, with their pockets stuffed with hundred-dollar bills, had been arrested after breaking into the Democratic National Committee's headquarters at the Watergate Hotel in Washington, D.C. All hands were called into the paper's office, where eight sea-soned reporters were assigned to the story. Woodward volunteered to help on it as well.

As a story started to gel, some of the information received appeared so outlandish that it bordered on the unbelievable. In the meantime, communications out of the White House downplayed the events in public as unimportant and unconnected to the Nixon adminis-tration, while in private high-ranking officials called the FBI in an attempt to quash the investigation. When the story first broke, Woodward naturally called Felt for information, but Felt was curt, gave him nothing to work with, and hung up. Woodward found his way to Felt's home, where the FBI's second-in-command agreed to help, albeit with severely mixed feelings. He insisted, though, that they take precautions straight out of a spy novel. If Woodward wanted to meet, he would place a red flag in the flower pot sitting in a window of his home, in which case they would meet at 2:00 a.m. the next morning. If Felt wanted a meeting, Woodward would find page 20 of his copy of the New York Times circled with clock hands drawn on the page to show what time the meeting would be (Woodward never discovered how Felt got access to his copy of the paper). They would then each proceed to an underground parking garage in Rosslyn, a suburb of Washington, D.C., at the appointed hour. Even then, Felt instructed Woodward to drive a car other than his own, to take alleys instead of main streets, and to walk the last several blocks to the garage.

Felt never supplied information directly, but would confirm or deny the accuracy of leads the Post dug up and would hint at avenues to pursue, leaving it to Woodward to figure things out from there. In this way, the Post uncovered an unprecedented level of corruption in the White House. Only a few members of the Post knew the identity of the secret source who came to be known as "Deep Throat," a reference both to his deep cover and the name of a pornographic film popular at the time. Attorney General John Mitchell controlled a secret fund that was used to pay people to spy on the Democrats, while other aides to President Nixon conducted a massive campaign of political spying and sabotage. Eventually over thirty people pleaded guilty or were convicted of crimes such as perjury, burglary, wiretapping, and obstruction of justice, including White House staff members, its legal counsel, the special counsel to the President, and members of the Committee to Reelect the President.

ः   ः   ः

As the members of his inner circle began to fall like dominoes, the heat on Richard Nixon escalated. The final straw was the discovery of damaging audiotapes Nixon made of discussions between himself and members of his staff. Three days after transcripts of the tapes were released to the public in August of 1974, the 37th President of the United States announced his resignation. One month later his hand-picked successor, Gerald Ford, pardoned Nixon for any crimes he may have committed while he was President.

The Washington Post *won a Pulitzer Prize for its coverage of the Watergate scandal.* All the President's Men, *the 1976 movie based on Woodward's telling of his and Carl Bernstein's efforts in uncovering the facts of Watergate, was nominated for a Best Picture Oscar. Jason Robards won the award as Best Supporting Actor for his role as* Washington Post *editor Ben Bradlee.*

The identity of Deep Throat was a closely held secret for decades and inspired much specula-tion. Felt was identified as the source in 2005.

Parking spot number 32 on level D of The Oakhill Office Building, where Bob Woodward and Mark Felt met six times. The building was torn down in 2017.

20

1907 | Art School Reject

A.H. HAD LITTLE USE FOR *school, and either his lack of interest or a limited grasp of the subject matter led to his being held back a grade twice. Things did not improve by the time he made it to high school. While he excelled in German and art, his performance in other subjects was poor to average, and he was marked as "Unsatisfactory" in French and Mathematics. He had only one friend as a boy, and even that so-called friend would later remember A.H. as "violent and high strung." Academically challenged and unpopular with the other students, A.H. dropped out of school in 1905. For the next few years he led an aimless life, sleeping late, wandering around his hometown of Linz, Austria, with occasional visits to a museum or an opera performance, and then staying up late reading and drawing.*

A.H. did have some talent at art, and during his late-night sketching sessions would dream of becoming a great artist. With this in mind, he traveled to Vienna, Austria, which around the turn of the twentieth century was establishing itself as a mecca for free-thinking artists who pushed styles in new and exciting directions. Some of the greatest painters, composers, and architects of the time gathered there and found acceptance and inspiration in the city. Convinced that he belonged among that elite crowd, in 1907 A.H. applied for a place in the prestigious Vienna Academy of Fine Arts, where he was invited to sit for the two-day entrance exam for the school of painting. It did not even occur to A.H. that there was a chance he would not be admitted.

The staff members judging his works were not impressed with his submissions on the exam, finding that he had a lack of talent for artistic painting, particularly when it came to the human form. A.H. was stunned by the rejection and left Vienna to return home. While there, he received another blow when his mother took ill and died. Unsure of what other options he may have, A.H. returned to Vienna, intending to retake the exam for the Academy's 1908 entry class. While scraping by taking odd jobs such as shoveling snow for wealthy homeowners, A.H. reached out to a friend of his mother, a stage designer of some note, who arranged for a letter of recommendation expressing admiration for his artistic ability. This time, however, the school turned him down without even giving him the opportunity to sit for the entrance exam. Even A.H. knew then that a place in the Academy was not to be and he did not try again.

In 1913, A. H. left Austria to avoid arrest for evading his obligation to serve in the Austrian military, settling in Munich, Germany, where he continued to lead a directionless existence, subsisting on the sale of an occasional watercolor painting. With the outbreak of World War

I, however, he signed on with the German army. He was wounded twice in battle, achieved the rank of Lance Corporal, and came out of the war with four medals. More important, he was apparently exposed to radical political views at that time, which were to shape his own thinking and eventually lead to entire world into another war.

ଔ   ଔ   ଔ

Adolf Hitler's rejection from art school not only loosed one of history's most vicious dictators upon the world, contributing to millions of casualties in World War II, but also played a role in his attitude toward the Jewish race. He blamed Jewish teachers at the Vienna Academy for unfairly judging his artistic abilities and denying him a place in the school. His mother's death, he felt, was due to the incompetence of Jewish doctors. Shoveling snow and performing other tasks he felt were demeaning for wealthy citizens of Vienna, whom Hitler assumed were Jewish, also grated, and planted the thought in his mind that the aristocracy that held the people back were all Jewish. One can only wonder how events would have been different if young Hitler's attentions had been focused on painting instead of politics.

& *Hitler's artworks have been macabre collectors' items. In 2015, fourteen of his paintings, watercolors, and drawings brought in $450,000.00 at auction, with one item alone selling for around $112,500.00.*

"The Courtyard of the Old Residency in Munich"
by Adolf Hitler, 1914

21

Lucky Breaks That Made Careers That Affected Us All

JOSEPH PULITZER

During the Civil War, Northerners with the means to pay for it were allowed to hire a substitute to serve in their place in the Union Army. This practice led to a proliferation of bounty hunters whose job it was to find volunteers to fight for these wealthy men, and many of the hunters went to Europe to find replacement soldiers. In this way, seventeen-year-old Hungarian citizen Joseph Pulitzer signed a contract to serve in place of a draftee.

After fulfilling his duties with a year in the Lincoln Cavalry, Pulitzer was unable to find a steady job and made do as a part-time muleteer, baggage handler, and waiter. In his spare time he went to the library to study English and the law, as well as to play chess in a room the library had set aside for that purpose. While watching a match between two men he had never met, he impressed the players with his astute commentary about one of their moves. The players were editors of a local German-language newspaper, and without so much as the benefit of an interview, offered Pulitzer a job as a junior reporter.

Four years later, when the paper experienced financial difficulties, Pulitzer was offered the chance to buy a controlling interest in it. Using funds from his Civil War bounty, he did so, and thus became a publisher at the young age of 25. He turned the paper's fortunes around and in the process became well-off financially. He subsequently bought the *St. Louis Post-Dispatch* and, later, the *New York World*. His position as editor and owner brought with it both wealth and power, and Pulitzer became one of the most influential people in America, as well as a noted philanthropist.

Before he died, Pulitzer endowed the fund with which the Pulitzer Prize is associated today. In addition, he spearheaded the drive to raise money for the pedestal that supports the Statue of Liberty. All because of a chess match.

NANCY AND RONALD REAGAN

In the fall of 1949, aspiring actor Anne Frances Robbins, working under the screen name Nancy Davis, had her first film role in the MGM production of *Shadow on the Wall*. She was astonished and upset one morning while reading a Hollywood newspaper to find her name on a list of Communist sympathizers, which in the witch-hunt atmosphere of the Joseph McCarthy era could lead to being blacklisted and never being able to work in movies again.

In fact, the newspaper list alluded to another actor of the same name who had a reputation as appearing in "leftist" theater productions and whose name was on a petition to the United States Supreme Court attempting to overturn the contempt of court arrest of two screenwriters who had refused to cooperate with McCarthy's House Un-American Activities Committee. Concerned, Davis asked her director to reach out to the President of the Screen Actors Guild, Ronald Reagan, to clarify the matter and to clear her name.

Reagan promised that he would intervene if any problems arose. Unsatisfied, Davis insisted on meeting Reagan to discuss the matter further. Reagan, encouraged by director Mervyn LeRoy's suggestion that he take Davis out for dinner, did so. The meeting turned into a date, which included dinner and an impromptu show, and the stage, so to speak, was set. They married in 1952. Nancy Reagan was a huge influence in her husband's entry into politics; without her, it is unlikely that Ronald Reagan would ever have been elected President of the United States.

Engagement photograph of Nancy Davis and Ronald Reagan, 1952

J.K. Rowling

Rowling first had the idea for the Harry Potter books while sitting on a delayed train while traveling to London in 1990. Over the next several years she planned and plotted the series on scraps of paper before sitting down to write it. By that time, she was the divorced single mother of a baby girl.

Rowling sent the first three chapters of what was to become *Harry Potter and the Philosopher's Stone* to one editor after another. All of them, about twelve in total, rejected her, some in not-so-kind terms. Her last chance, as she saw it, was Bloomsbury Publishing, where it fell into the hands of Nigel Newton to determine the manuscript's fate. Instead of reading it himself, Newton gave the first chapter to his eight-year-old daughter Alice. An hour later, Alice emerged from her room proclaiming to her dad that "this is so much better than anything else" and demanding the next chapter. Over the next month she continued to nag her father to see what came next, which led to the publisher agreeing to take on Harry Potter.

As of 2011, over 450 million Harry Potter books had been sold in at least 68 different languages, and the movies based on the novels have grossed more than $7.7 billion.

LERNER AND LOWE

The team of Alan Jay Lerner and Frederick Loewe are responsible for some of the world's best-loved musicals, including *Paint Your Wagon, My Fair Lady, Gigi,* and *Camelot*, but their partnership began when Loewe got lost looking for the bathroom. Lerner was dining at the Lamb's Club in New York in August of 1942 at a time when he was in the market for a new composer to pair music with his lyrics. As described in his own words, a "short, well built, tightly strung man with a large head and hands and immensely dark circles under his eyes" began to pass by Lerner's table before stopping short. The man, of course, was Loewe, who was looking for the men's room but had gone the wrong way, which brought him into the room where Lerner was dining. Loewe recognized Lerner and invited himself to sit down.

The two men agreed to team up. Their first three efforts at a musical were failures, but after that they wrote a string of successes that is nearly unparalleled. When it first hit the stage in 1956, *My Fair Lady* set a record for the number of Broadway performances.

Julie Andrews as Eliza Doolittle in the original
Broadway production of *My Fair Lady*, 1957

22

Duel #3
1864 | The Duel That Never Was

I N THE LATE 1850s, VIRGINIA *City, Nevada, was a sleepy Western town of barely two thousand residents, many of them miners seeking their fortune in gold. It was to be a different precious metal, however, that brought an onslaught of would-be millionaires from around the world, increasing the local population tenfold by 1874. In 1857, brothers Evan and Hosea Grosh found a deposit of silver, but both men died before they could record their claim. That honor fell to Henry Comstock, a gold prospector and part-time sheepherder who had watched over the Groshes' cabin. Apparently not realizing the extent of the deposit, Comstock sold the mining rights and ended up dying a poor man.*

The discovery bore his name, however, and the "Comstock Lode" ended up being the richest silver deposit in United States history. Virginia City transformed from a little-known mudhole to a thriving metropolis (by Western standards). At its peak, it boasted a six-story hotel that had the only elevator west of Chicago, along with 110 saloons, numerous opium dens, and twenty theaters and dance halls. Everyone, of course, was well-armed.

Into this madness arrived S.C., a journalist who had taken the position of typesetter at the Territorial Enterprise *for a salary of twenty-five dollars per week. The newspaper had the reputation of not only being one of the most spirited in the country, but one that held little regard for the truthfulness of its stories. Its goal was to sell papers, and the flexibility this offered S.C. suited him just fine. It also nearly got him killed.*

Quickly rising from typesetter to reporter, S.C. found a talent for writing colorful pieces of semi-fiction that passed as truth in the Territorial. *In this vein, as acting editor while the paper's editor was out of town, he accused a rival paper,* The Daily Union, *of reneging on a charitable bid for a sack of flour. He decided not to publish the satirical piece and set it aside. A typesetter found the document, however, and assumed it was meant to be included in the next issue. And so it was.*

The backlash from The Daily Union *was fierce. Accusations and insults flew back and forth in the respective papers until at one point S.C.'s manliness was questioned. This was the last straw for S.C., and he demanded a retraction from James Laird, the editor of the rival publication. Laird refused. Against his better judgment, S.C. challenged Laird to a duel, hoping that he would decline. At first Laird did, but S.C., egged on by other employees of the* Territorial, *continued to issue ever more insulting challenges. Finally Laird accepted.*

It was rash behavior on the part of S.C., who was completely inept at firing a pistol. Laird, on the other hand, was reputed (by S.C.'s own account) to be able to hit his mark 13 out of every 18 times, a remarkable record given the inaccuracy of weapons of that time. Given that a lack of manliness was the insult precipitating the challenge, S.C. could hardly back out.

On the day of the duel, S.C. and his second arrived at the chosen location early for shooting practice. The second placed a squash roughly the size of a human head on top of a barn door as a target. S.C. not only could not hit the fruit, he couldn't hit the barn door. Noting his futility, the second took out his frustration at a small passing bird sitting on a bush thirty paces away, shooting his own weapon at it and taking off its head. At that very moment Laird's second arrived, noting the result but not the act itself. Inquiring who shot the bird from that distance, he was told that it had been S.C. Laird's second rushed back to Laird, reported the incident, and the duel was called off.

ଔ   ଔ   ଔ

Perhaps not wanting to push his luck, Samuel Clemens—who first used his pen name Mark Twain in a piece published in the *Territorial Enterprise*—left Virginia City shortly after the "Duel That Never Was." He went on to use the humorous and irreverent style that first became evident in his writings for the newspaper to author some of this country's best and most popular novels, including *A Connecticut Yankee in King Arthur's Court, Tom Sawyer,* and *The Adventures of Huckleberry Finn*. One of his earlier books, *Roughing It* (1872), drew heavily on his adventures in the West, including his time in Virginia City. While it appears clear that the challenge to a duel between Twain and Laird was issued, the details of what happened after that are less clear. Almost the only source of the bird story is Twain himself, and given his propensity for

Young firemen pose on the streets of Virginia City, 1862

embellishment we can only wonder if it truly happened that way.

The Nevada Historical Society wants to believe that it did. Its collection contains a rusty, fire-damaged portion of a pistol that it received in 1910, at the time purported to be Twain's pistol from the duel. While it is from the correct time period, there is no definitive proof whether it did or did not belong to the author.

23

Accidental Scientific Discoveries
in the Earth and Sky

I T SEEMS ALMOST COMMONPLACE FOR *construction workers to unearth a lost city or for a farmer to find ancient artifacts while plowing a field. Diligent research and a dash of expert guesswork can often lead to an important discovery, but pure chance has played a significant role as well. Here is a small sampling of accidental discoveries found under the ground and out in space.*

ARCHAEOLOGY
1709 ~ Herculaneum

While the city of Pompeii gets most of the publicity and the hordes of tourists, it was not the only city covered by ash when Mount Vesuvius erupted in 79 A.D. Herculaneum, a somewhat more wealthy community of about four thousand residents, was upwind from the volcano, so it had an additional twelve hours before the blistering shower of ash and volcanic gas buried the city. Its existence was known, but no one actually found it until a farmer digging a deep well unearthed statuary and other items from what was eventually identified as the city's theater. Today, much of the city has been uncovered and it is a UNESCO World Heritage site.

Skeletons in a Herculaneum boathouse

1820 ~ Venus De Milo

Venus De Milo. This easily recognizable marble statue of Aphrodite, absent her arms, was originally carved in Greece around 150 B.C., but at some later point was lost and its existence forgotten. It wasn't until nearly two millennia later that she emerged from hiding, when a farmer removing stones from a niche in a stone wall on the Aegean island of Melos found pieces of her body. The statue is currently on display at the Louvre Museum in Paris, where it is considered a "must-see."

Alexandros's Venus de Milo
in the Lourvre

1940 ~ The Lascaux Caves

Four teenagers chasing an errant dog in the French countryside near Montignac followed the curious canine into a cavern and discovered more than the dog. Inside was a complex of caves whose walls were decorated with some six hundred paintings of animals, including horses, rhinoceroses, and mythical beasts (but only one human), and fifteen hundred engravings. The artwork is estimated to be around fifteen to twenty thousand years old and represents some of the Paleolithic era's finest examples.

Painting from the Lascaux Caves

1997 ~ The Lyceum

Plato established the Western world's first university in ancient Greece, but it was his star pupil Aristotle who founded a school of philosophy in the Lyceum temple in 335 B.C.

Its location was lost over time, and archeologists' efforts to find it over a period of a hundred years failed. Workers in downtown Athens preparing a construction site for the National Museum of Contemporary Art eventually uncovered the ancient complex, complete with a central citadel and gymnasium,

Lyceum excavation in Athens

under an unpaved parking lot. The museum site was moved slightly to allow the Lyceum to become a permanent exhibit, which opened to the public in 2009.

2012 ~ Ruins of Serdica

Engineers excavating a subway line in downtown Sofia, the capital of Bulgaria, found remains of the ancient city of Serdica, a thriving metropolis in early Roman times, where Constantine the Great once lived while searching for a location to establish the capital city for his empire. Among the discoveries were colorful floor mosaics, early sewage systems, and a private bathhouse. Today this site is home to an open-air museum. Since 2012, construction of the subway has unearthed many more portions of Serdica, although not all have been preserved as carefully. Some metro stations in Sofia have displays of artifacts uncovered during construction of the subway.

East gate of Serdica in the subway of Sofia, Bulgaria

PALEONTOLOGY
1856 ~ The Neanderthal

German workers quarrying limestone unearthed bones in a cave. Thinking they were the remains of a bear, they tossed the bones aside. Only after the skullcap was brought to a schoolteacher, who passed them on to the University of Bonn, were they identified as a new species of hominid, the Neanderthal.

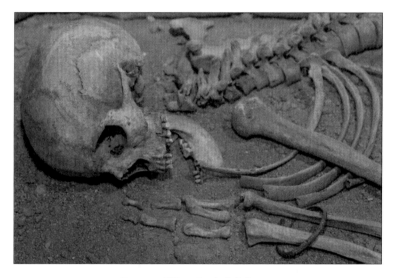

Excavated Neanderthal skeleton

1868 ~ Cro-Magnons

Workers clearing a path for a new road in southern France exposed the entrance to a limestone rock shelter, where they found skeletal remains of four adult and one infant *homo sapiens,* along with stone tools and perforated beads. The finding was the first known example of Cro-Magnons.

1921 ~ First-Known Ancestor of Modern Humans

Miners extracting iron and zinc in Zambia, Africa, accidentally came upon bones dating to 125,000–300,000 years ago, which turned out to be the first-known common ancestor of Neanderthals and modern humans.

1947 ~ Dead Sea Scrolls

A Bedouin shepherd and his cousin looking for a lost lamb along the north shore of the Dead Sea stumbled upon jars in a cave, some of which contained documents made of animal skin or papyrus. Ultimately a collection of over eight hundred Biblical texts dating from 2000 B.C. to 70 A.D., the oldest in existence, were brought out of the cave and became known as the Dead Sea Scrolls.

Portion of the Dead Sea Scrolls

The cave of Qumran, where the scrolls were discovered

1997 ~ Coelacanth

Coelacanth fish

A graduate student in marine biology was on his honeymoon exploring an Indonesian fish market when his wife pointed to a large, strange-looking fish at one of the stalls. Showing that the money spent on his education was not a waste, the student identified the fish as a previously unknown species of coelacanth, a rare type of fish closely resembling fossils of fish that swam the seas 400 million years ago. At that time, it was believed that coelacanths had been extinct for 66 million years.

2001 ~ Civilization of the Four Lakes

An electric company in southern Greece, excavating a mine looking for lignite, instead found the remains of fifty-four ancient settlements, including buildings, tools, pottery, jewelry, clay figurines, and a necropolis containing 148 tombs at last count. The discovery has been named the "Civilization of the Four Lakes."

2016 ~ Ancient Mosaic & Roman Villa

Luke Irwin, a well-known rug designer living in Wiltshire, England, was laying electric cable in his barn when he discovered an ancient mosaic underground. That was only the beginning, as his land was sitting on top of a three-story-high Roman villa dating back to around 175 to 220 A.D. Irwin later designed a series of rugs modeled after the mosaic.

ASTRONOMY
1963 ~ Gamma Rays from Space

At the height of the Cold War, the U.S., the United Kingdom and the U.S.S.R. entered into an agreement putting a moratorium on the testing of nuclear weapons. Ever distrustful, the U.S. Air Force launched spy satellites to look for any violations, which would be evidenced by the presence of gamma rays and X-rays emanating from the Earth below. What they discovered instead were gamma rays that were coming *from* space. This was the first detection of these waves from space, which contain the most energy of any along the electromagnetic scale, and which emanate from supernova explosions and regions near black holes.

1964 ~ The Big Bang Buzz

Bell Laboratory employees Arno Penzias and Robert Wilson were using a funnel-shaped antenna to collect radio waves as a way of keeping tabs on the company's balloon satellites. No matter which direction they pointed the antenna, however, they were bothered by an annoying buzzing sound. Thinking the buzz came from interference caused by pigeons nesting in the cone, they shooed the birds away. The buzzing persisted, and led to the discovery that the scientists were hearing the soft hiss left over from the Big Bang, the explosion that formed the Universe.

2013 ~ New Magnetar

Scientists confidently predicted that a particular gas cloud would be ripped apart by a black hole, and trained their telescopes into space in anticipation. Months later, they were still waiting. What their telescopes did pick up, however, was the brightest X-ray flash ever seen, 400 times brighter than its background star, which evidenced a new magnetar, a rare kind of neutron star, which they only saw because they were looking for something else.

GEOLOGY
1898 ~ Carlsbad Caverns

The Carlsbad Caverns

James Larkin White dropped out of school at the age of ten to become a cowboy and moved to a ranch in New Mexico to fulfill his dream. Six years later, while out looking for stray cattle in the Chihuahuan Desert, White saw what he at first thought was a tornado or whirlwind of some kind. Curious, he moved closer to find that what he was seeing was a large colony of bats coming out of the hills. Looking for the source of the bats, he found what he called "the biggest and blackest hole I had ever seen." This hole became known as Carlsbad Caverns, one of the oldest cave systems in the world. It consists of a huge complex of 119 caves containing seventeen species of bats and hosts about a quarter of a million visitors annually.

24

1914 | A Wrong Turn Brings the World to War

ON ITS SURFACE, EUROPE IN *the early years of the twentieth century was enjoying a* *period of both idyllic peace and booming prosperity. Commerce was flourishing and* *manufacturing was expanding at unprecedented rates. New products were being intro-* *duced to the world at such a pace it was hard to keep up with the latest trends, and popula-* *tion across the continent was expanding at a rapid pace. The thriving economy relied on* *cooperation among the various nations of Europe, which also found common ground to* *come to terms in addressing international issues such as controlling the spread of disease,* *trade, working conditions, and white slavery. Travel across borders for reasons other than* *business was no longer just for the wealthy, as middle-class citizens began to discover the* *pleasures of tourism. The general feeling at the time, and the opinion of many contempo-* *rary commentators, was that war was a virtual impossibility.*

Underneath this seemingly tranquil environment, however, simmered pockets of intense *dissatisfaction and unrest. Most conflicts that came to the surface were settled through the* *traditional means of diplomacy and restraint, helped by a lack of political will to enter into* *war. Nothing, though, placated Serbian nationalists, who were enraged when the province of* *Bosnia was annexed by Austria-Hungary in 1908 instead of becoming part of the indepen-* *dent Serbian state. Inevitably radical groups formed, with the goal of bringing Bosnia under* *Serbian rule by any means possible.*

Into this picture enters Archduke *Ferdinand, heir to the Austro-* *Hungarian Empire, who travelled to* *Sarajevo, in the heart of Bosnia, on* *June 28, 1914, to inspect his troops.* *His choice of date was precipitous,* *as it was not only his wedding anni-* *versary but the anniversary of a* *battle in 1389 that eventually led* *to Serbia's loss of independence, a* *date with substantial meaning to* *the Serbs. Despite warnings not to* *come, Ferdinand not only traveled*

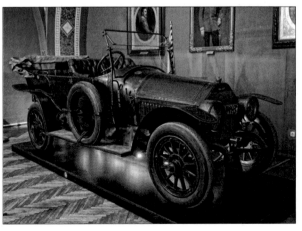

The automobile in which Ferdinand was shot

to Sarajevo, but moved about the city with his wife at his side in an open car made conspicuous by its bright red color.

A ragtag group of seven militant students, armed with guns and hand grenades supplied by the head of Serbian military intelligence, were spread out along his well-publicized route. As the Archduke's car came into view, one student lost his nerve and disappeared into the crowd. A second threw a grenade, but it bounced off of Ferdinand's car and only wounded members of his entourage. Discouraged and in a panic, the students disbursed quickly and avoided capture.

The incident may have ended there but for a remarkable event of chance. Forty-five minutes after the initial attempt on his life, still traveling in an open car, Ferdinand decided to visit the wounded members of his entourage in the hospital. Once away from the prearranged route, his driver got lost and began to turn down the wrong street. Immediately aware of his error, the driver slammed on his brakes to back up, but stalled the engine and caused the gears to lock up.

Incredibly, the car stalled in front of a café where one of the rebellious students, Gavrilo Princip, was consoling himself after the failed assassination with drink. Realizing what was happening, he immediately headed for the street. Hemmed in by a curious crowd, Princip was unable to pull the bomb still in his possession out of his pocket, so instead he aimed his pistol in the general direction of the car, from about five feet away. Despite the fact that he had no training in weapons, and that the pistols of the time were notoriously inaccurate and difficult to aim even by experienced marksmen, his two shots hit the Archduke and his wife, killing them both.

The assassination of the heir to the throne naturally enraged Austria, which submitted a list of demands as recompense to Serbia. Serbia agreed to most of them and for a moment it appeared that conflict had been avoided, but guided by emotion more than reason, Austria declared war on Serbia on July 28. In support of its neighbor, Russia mobilized forces to attack Austria, which caused Germany, a friend of Austria, to declare war on Russia. A series of other pacts between nations brought Belgium, France, and Great Britain, as well as other European nations, into battle. World War I, the "Great War," had begun.

ଓ   ଓ   ଓ

Over 17 million people died in World War I, including seven million civilians, but the death toll doesn't stop there. Many scholars believe that World War II would not have happened but for the first war. The treaty to end the World War I in 1918 contained terms that so humiliated Germany that it led to the rise of German nationalism, a perfect incubator for the dogma of Adolf Hitler.

According to legend, the vehicle in which Ferdinand and his wife met their demise became cursed, so that subsequent owners all met their maker by violent means while traveling in the car. While this tale appears not to be true, another mysterious fact involving the license plate of the car does seem to be supported by evidence. The plate number AIII 118 may have foreshadowed the day the Great War ended. Under this theory, the "A" stands for "Armistice," while the following numbers, broken into 11-11-18, reflect the official last date of the war, recognized as Armistice Day.

Archduke Ferdinand and his wife in the death car
shortly before their assassination

25

Accidental Inventions | Toy Edition

SILLY PUTTY

The serious endeavor of helping the war effort in World War II led to the development of a product that is hard to take seriously. In 1943, there was a severe shortage of natural rubber because Japan controlled most of the territories where rubber trees grew, and the Allies were desperate to find a substitute to use in making tires. James Wright and his team at General Electric worked long hours to produce a synthetic rubber that could withstand the high heat of jet engines as well as the freezing nights while sitting on Navy ships at sea. For over a year they experimented with endless combinations of chemical compounds.

One day in late summer, Wright added what he thought was boron nitride to a silicone oil. The experiment failed, but it turned out that the bottle had been mislabeled and was in fact a mixture of chemicals that included boric acid. With new optimism, Wright tried again with just boric acid. This new combination failed as well: it tended

Early advertisements for Silly Putty

to melt and wouldn't hold its shape. Frustrated, Wright threw the goopy mass on the floor, only to have it bounce back up to him. While the substance would be of no use to the military, Wright did recognize its potential as a novelty, and Silly Putty was born.

      The General Electric team did eventually create a synthetic rubber. As for Silly Putty, it was originally marketed to adults and was slow to catch on with the public. A creative marketing consultant finally put it into the familiar colorful plastic eggs and released them just before Easter, and also created one of the first television commercials aimed at children. Silly Putty has been popular ever since, selling over 300 million eggs since 1950. The same formula created inadvertently by James Wright is still used.

CHEWING GUM

People have been chewing gum of some sort for thousands of years. The ancient Greeks chewed on a plant-derived substance called mastic. Early Scandinavian cultures used birch bark tar or pitch. In North and Central America, the Maya and Aztecs both made use of chicle, the resin of sapodilla trees that formed a protective layer over any cuts in the bark. The Maya cooked and dried it into what they called *cha*, which supposedly quenched thirst and staved off hunger. The Aztecs used it as a breath freshener.

Adams' Gum advertisement

These early forms of gum were an acquired taste and bore little resemblance to modern chewing gum. For that we can thank Thomas Adams, Sr. and, indirectly, exiled Mexican President Antonio López de Santa Anna, who also led the Mexican forces at the Alamo. Santa Anna took a supply of chicle to Adams, asking him to develop a cheaper alternative to rubber, with which the former General hoped to earn a fortune that would help him buy his way back into the Mexican government's good graces.

Adams and his sons tried vulcanizing the chicle into a form of rubber and in the process attempted to make toys, masks, and rain boots. All were failures. Santa Ana abandoned the project, but Adams persisted. Eventually he too gave up, but then, remembering the history of chicle south of the border, rolled one of his failed chicle mixtures into balls, added flavoring, and found that the resulting chewable gum was far superior to the paraffin-based gums of that time. Anticipating a public demand, he formed a company specializing in the manufacture of chewing gum. In the 1870s he sold a sour orange-flavored gum as an after-dinner candy as well as a licorice-flavored line called "Black Jack." In 1888 he sold a Tutti-Frutti flavor in the first-ever chewing gum vending machines. By that time, Adams was manufacturing five tons of gum daily. Chewing gum had found its market and has never looked back.

In the early 1890s, a young soap salesman named William Wrigley tried to increase sales of his product by offering free gum to vendors who placed a large order for soap. The gum turned out to be more popular than the soap, and Wrigley changed focus. Juicy Fruit and Spearmint were introduced in 1893 and 1894. Today Wrigley holds 35 percent of the chewing gum market.

Gum companies today have strayed from the traditional flavors. Wrigley itself has offered mint chocolate chip ice cream-flavored gum. Other companies' flavors include meatball, dill pickle, bacon, wasabi, and foie gras. For Thanksgiving, be sure to try the three-flavor pack of turkey, cranberry, and pumpkin pie.

SLINKY

We have the military to thank once again for another popular toy, the Slinky. In 1943, at the same time James Wright's initial failures to produce an artificial rubber gave us Silly Putty, mechanical engineer Richard James worked in his lab at the Cramp Shipyard devising springs that could keep sensitive equipment steady on ships in roiling seas. Accidentally knocking some of his efforts off a high shelf, he watched in amazement as one of the springs took steps across his desk, down a stack of books, and onto the floor. He took the coil home to amuse his young son, who repeatedly sent it on trips down their long stairway. Soon all the neighborhood children wanted one of their own, and the Slinky toy was born. James spent whatever spare time he had over the next two years working to find the exact right type of wire and proper tension to perfect the product, then borrowed five hundred dollars from a friend to manufacture the first set of toys.

Sales were slow, even after Gimbels Department Store in Philadelphia agreed to make them part of a Christmas toy display alongside the dolls and electric train sets that were popular at the time. Wright and his wife Betty convinced Gimbels to allow them to demonstrate the toy in their store, and within minutes they had sold all of the hundred Slinkys they had brought with them, at a cost of a dollar apiece. The couple frantically sent for the remaining three hundred toys in their stock; those too were quickly snapped up and a large

Slinky advertisements

crowd waving dollar bills in their hands was clamoring for more. By Christmas Day, twenty thousand more units had been sold and the Slinky had established itself as a staple in the children's toy market.

James eventually gave away most of his fortune to ultra-conservative religious groups and then moved to Brazil to join a Christian cult, nearly driving his business to close. Betty took over the company, turned its fortunes around, and is responsible for the continued existence of Slinkys today.

> *What walks down stairs alone or in pairs and makes a slinky sound?*
> *A spring, a spring, a marvelous thing. Everyone knows it's Slinky.*
> *It's Slinky, it's Slinky, for fun it's a wonderful toy*
> *It's Slinky, it's Slinky, it's fun for a girl or a boy.*
>
> *~Early advertising jingle for Slinky*

PLAY-DOH

In the late 1920s, not long before the Great Depression, a Cincinnati, Ohio, soap company named Kutol was struggling and about to go out of business. In a last-ditch effort to stay afloat, it tasked 21-year-old Cleo McVicker to sell off whatever assets it had (mostly powdered soap)

to raise cash. The ploy succeeded—barely—and the company lived to see another day. Cleo then hired his brother Noah to market the products and help Kutol move forward.

In 1933, Cleo met with representatives of the Kroger grocery chain in an effort to place its soap on the store shelves. Asked if Kutol made wallpaper cleaner, a necessity to remove soot from walls in homes heated by coal, Cleo replied that it did and Kroger immediately ordered fifteen thousand cases. In fact, Kutol did *not* manufacture wallpaper cleaner at the time and had no formula for doing so. The brothers managed to develop one that was non-toxic, reusable and that wouldn't stain the wallpaper, and Kutol survived another challenge.

Kutol wallpaper cleaner before it became Play-Doh

By the mid-1940s, demand for wallpaper cleaner fell as oil and gas heat replaced coal, and fell further as vinyl wallpaper, easily cleaned with soap and water, came onto the market. To make matters worse for Kutol, Cleo died in an airplane accident in 1949. Cleo's son Joe McVicker was hired to replace him.

The company struggled to survive but was still around in 1954, when Joe's sister-in-law Kay Zufall needed cheap materials for her nursery school students to make Christmas decorations. She happened to read a magazine article that suggested using wallpaper cleaner, and immediately ran out to buy some Kutol product. Her kids loved playing with it, and she called Joe.

Joe removed the detergent from the cleaner and added almond scent and coloring. Kay came up with the name "Play-Doh" (rejecting Joe's idea of "Kutol's Rainbow Modeling Compound") and the two began selling the product to schools in the Cincinnati area. Looking to expand the market, Joe managed to get onto the set of the Captain Kangaroo television show. Bob Keeshan, who played the Captain, agreed to use Play-Doh on the set of the show at least once every week in return for two percent of the sales. Sales skyrocketed, and Play-Doh was here to stay.

 Play-Doh is easy to make at home: combine two cups of flour, two cups of warm water, one cup of salt, two tablespoons vegetable oil, one tablespoon cream of tartar, and liquid food coloring.

26

1839 | That's How the (Rubber) Ball Bounces

RUBBER, IN ITS RAW FORM *derived from a tree found mainly in Brazil, has been used for varied purposes for centuries. The earliest written reference to it came from a member of an expedition led by explorer Hernán Cortés, who in 1511 observed a native Aztec tribe playing with a rubber ball and marveled at the way it would bounce back up after hitting the ground. It took another three centuries to catch on, but by the early 1800s, companies were rushing to take advantage of its uniquely flexible features and imported "gum elastic" from South America by the barrel-full in an effort to get products using this miracle substance to market. The first rubber factory was established in England in 1820 and seemingly hundreds of competitors soon joined the fray, including the Roxbury India Rubber Company of Boston, the first such venture in the United States.*

Rubber-based products, including overcoats, shoes, and boots, began flying out of factories and into customers' homes. Unfortunately for companies in the U.S., rubber is very fickle when it comes to temperature changes. While the moderate climate of Great Britain hid this unstable side of rubber, the extreme temperatures of North America exposed the problem in a most unfortunate way. In high heat, rubber melts into a gelatinous goo, while in cold temperatures it becomes brittle and cracks. Furious consumers of boots that broke in the winter and melted in the summer returned their purchases to the factories. Within only a few years, the rubber boom dissolved and all but a handful of companies went out of business. Investors lost millions of dollars and thousands of workers lost their jobs. Roxbury itself survived, but was on life support as it struggled to find a solution to the problem.

At this very point in time a hardware proprietor and part-time inventor from Philadelphia, who as a schoolboy had become fascinated by the mysterious properties of rubber, happened to be walking by the Roxbury store and stopped dead when he saw its window display of life preservers, for which he had an obsession. C.G. entered the store, purchased a preserver and took it home, where he quickly devised an ingenious improvement to the preserver's valve. Traveling back to Boston, he showed it to the owner of Roxbury, expecting to strike a deal for his valve. Instead, he was treated to the owner's sad tale of thirty thousand life preservers for which he'd had to issue refunds after they melted, bringing the company to the verge of bankruptcy. Rather than sell a valve to a struggling company, the owner suggested, why didn't C.G. find a way to stabilize rubber into a useable form?

With his own business near failure, C.G. returned to Philadelphia with a new mission in mind. Almost immediately he was arrested and thrown into jail for failing to make good on debts related to loans he had taken out to expand his hardware empire. Undeterred, he had his wife bring him a sample of the Brazilian rubber gum, which he experimented with in his cell as he tried to find a solution to its quirks. Upon his release, taming rubber became his single-minded pursuit, even as his family had to resort to digging up half-grown potatoes from the neighbor's yard to avoid starvation. Hoping to bring some money into the family coffers, he produced rubber overshoes in his kitchen. They melted. For years, the answer remained elusive.

Ever obsessive, C.G. often worked late into the night. Early one morning, running short of materials, he re-used an old sample he had painted with magnesium and quicklime to brighten the dingy color of rubber. As a preliminary, C.G. applied nitric acid to remove the paint, but to his disappointment the acid turned the sample black and he threw it away. A few days later, curiosity got to him and he pulled the sample from the garbage, only to find that the rubber was smooth and dry. Sure he was onto something, C.G. started a new business making mailbags out of the new substance and stored them in a warm place pending sale. They, too, dissolved. C.G. went broke, but kept trying.

One subsequent effort involved adding sulfur to the gum. On bringing his latest sample to the general store, he got agitated by the snickers from the other men, waved his arms excitedly, and watched helplessly as a fistful of the substance flew out of his hand and onto the hot potbellied stove. When he went to scrape it off, he found that instead of melting, the mixture had charred like leather and had a dry, springy rim. Inspired by the knowledge that heat and the addition of sulfur miraculously transformed rubber, he rushed home to experiment with different proportions of materials and various temperatures. When he finally found that steam under pressure for four to six hours at 270 degrees did the trick, Charles Goodyear had invented vulcanized rubber. The invention revolutionized industry.

CB   CB   CB

Contemporary newspapers of Woburn, Massachusetts, where the famous general store was located, insisted that the incident of the rubber sample hitting the stove happened as written above. Other papers of the time say that he was simply holding his hands out to warm them when he dropped the rubber. Still other versions attribute spilling sulfur onto a rubberized apron, dropping a bit of rubber and a sulfur match onto the stove, and attempting to hide a rubber-sulfur mixture from his wife by throwing it into his home stove before retrieving it later. In his memoirs, Goodyear admits the discovery was accidental, although in later years he bristled at the notion that it was anything but the product of his hard work and strong mind.

Despite patenting his invention, Goodyear never gained wealth from it. Poor health, more prison time, and competitors disregarding his patent left him $200,000.00 in debt when he died. The Goodyear Company was founded long after his death by two brothers whose only connection to Charles was an admiration for his work.

 Today, there is one cultivated rubber tree for every two people on Earth.

Rubber store advertisement from 1861

27

1989 | A Slip of the Tongue That Brought Down a Wall

WITH THE END OF WORLD War II in 1945, the victorious Allies were not always on the same page as to how to divide the spoils of war. The uneasy alliance between the Soviet Union and the Western powers such as the United States and Great Britain, fed by a general distrust of each other, led to some unusual compromises. One such result was the division of Germany into four zones, with the Eastern part of the country ceded to Soviet control and oversight of the Western section given to the United States, Great Britain, and France. The City of Berlin, despite being located in the heart of the Soviet's Eastern zone, was similarly split.

From the outset, the Soviets despised having such a conspicuously capitalistic city situated deep within the communist part of Germany. In an effort to drive out this island of Western influence, Russia did not wait long before attempting a blockade of food and other provisions into West Berlin. The U.S. and other countries air-dropped supplies into the citizens on the Western side of the city for nearly a year, breaking the blockade, and the Soviet Union gave up the effort. Tensions, however, remained high.

During this period, residents of the East (formally known as the German Democratic Republic, or "GDR") and West sides of Berlin freely crossed the porous border to work, shop and find entertainment at the theater. Train and subway lines extended both ways. For some East Berliners, though, a mere visit to the West was not enough. Between 1945 and 1961, about 2.5 million residents fled from the East to the West, reducing the GDR's population by an astonishing fifteen percent. Worse, many of those leaving were young, educated professionals, and skilled workers, causing a severe labor shortage. It was only a matter of time before the governments of the GDR and the Soviet Union took steps to stop the drain of talent.

That time came in 1961, in the early days of the administration of John F. Kennedy. The President had only been in office a few months when the Soviets sent cosmonaut Yuri Gagarin into space for ninety minutes, an accomplishment that stunned the world and gave the communist nation confidence in its place on the world stage. Just a few days later, in supporting an ill-advised and poorly planned attempt to overturn the Fidel Castro regime in Cuba, the U.S. nearly caused a war when the Bay of Pigs effort fell apart in a complete disaster. This too emboldened the Soviets and gave them reason to assume that world opinion was on their side and against the United States, the primary face of Western powers.

Meanwhile, the flight of German refugees to the West continued, and even picked up pace. Thirty thousand people fled the GDR in July of 1961 and eleven thousand more left in the *first eleven days of August. That night, shortly after midnight, the East Germans acted. A makeshift wall of barbed wire and concrete began to rise at the border, and within two weeks it was completed, extending completely across Berlin and into the countryside of Germany for almost a hundred miles. Streets, subway and rail lines, and even apartment houses were divided overnight, with sewers blocked and telephone lines cut. Over time, this temporary barrier was replaced with a twelve-foot high, four-foot wide mass of reinforced concrete, topped with an enormous pipe that made scaling the wall nearly impossible. On the Eastern side lay the so-called "Death Strip," a gauntlet of sand to make footprints easy to detect, along with floodlights, vicious dogs, and three hundred watchtowers manned with soldiers under instructions to shoot to kill anyone who attempted to cross.*

For twenty-eight years, the Berlin Wall remained a menacing structure preventing any more crossings. Some tried and a few made it over, but many more were killed trying. While the Wall showed no signs of giving way, the same might not have been said about the ruling party of the GDR. In 1989 civil unrest had spread even to East Berlin, with demonstrations by its citizens, demanding more freedom. A band of Communist reformers ousted the hardliners formerly in power and sought a way to quell the protests by projecting a new attitude toward change. With this in mind, they began to draft secret proposals to allow limited travel to the West with the idea of being hailed as heroes by the public. Such travel would still be restricted, requiring a lengthy application process and issuance of a visa. The length of stay would be limited to a maximum of thirty days, and permanent emigration was never contemplated.

Into this scenario came Günter Schabowski, an editor for a Communist party newspaper and an experienced propagandist. He was newly assigned to the role of party spokesman, which included holding televised news conferences for the ruling Politburo, a fairly new event in East Berlin. On the evening of November 9, 1989, Schabowski dropped by his boss's office on his way to the press conference and asked if there was anything new to report. He was handed a two-page memorandum outlining the upcoming loosening of the travel ban. Tired and distracted after a long day, he failed to read it carefully, and then held the information until the end of the conference. When he did announce the government's plan to open travel, he failed to note all of the restrictions and, in response to a question, wearily and erroneously reported that the effect of the new rules would take place immediately. In what his superior would later call a "botch," he gave the impression on live television that the borders were now open to cross.

ʘʘʘ ʘʘʘ ʘʘʘ

Within minutes, eighty East German citizens had already gathered at one of the checkpoints. The crowd soon swelled to the thousands, pushing forward in a mass toward the barrier. Without direction, unnerved, and in fear for the safety of his soldiers protecting the border, the checkpoint commander had his men step aside and the joyful throngs poured into West Berlin. Once started, the GDR was unable to stop the crossings and soon gave up even trying. Souvenir hunters began chipping off pieces of the wall, a process that the governments jointly completed in 1992.

 Germany was formally reunited in October of 1990. For his part in the collapse of the wall, Schabowski was expelled from the communist party.

Soviet tanks near Checkpoint Charlie (1961)

Sources & Resources

CHURCHILL

Gilbert, Martin. *Churchill: A Life.* New York: Henry Holt & Co, 1992. Print.

Shelden, Michael. *Young Titan: The Making of Winston Churchill.* New York: Simon & Schuster, 2013. Print.

Paterson, Michael. W*inston Churchill: Personal Accounts of the Great Leader at War.* Devon: David & Charles, 2005. Print.

Humes, James C. *Churchill: The Prophetic Statesman.* Washington, D.C.: Regnery History, 2012. Print.

Churchill, Randolph S. *Winston S. Churchill: Youth 1874-1900.* Boston: Houghton Mifflin & Company, 1966. Print.

"The Victorian School." *The Victorian School.* Paradox, 2009, 2010, 2011. Web.

Adenkan, Gafar. *The Grand Caliph: Recounting His Story and Glory: 7 Lessons All Leaders and Would-be Leaders Must Learn From Him.* Johannesburg: PartridgeAfrica, 2015. Print.

THEODORE GEISEL

"Who is Dr. Seuss?" *Seuss in Springfield.* Dr. Seuss Enterprises. 2017. Web.

Pease, Donald E. *Theodore Seuss Geisel: Lives and Legacy.* Oxford: Oxford University Press, 2010. Print.

Morgan, Judith and Neil. *Dr. Seuss and Mr. Geisel: A Biography.* New York: Random House, 1995. Print.

Wikipedia. "Dr. Seuss Bibliography." *Wikipedia, The Free Encyclopedia.* Wikipedia, The Free Encyclopedia. 2 May 2017. Web.

"How Dr. Seuss Got His Start 'On Mulberry Street.'" *Morning Edition.* National Public Radio, 24 Jan. 2012. Web.

"Mulberry Street May Fade, but 'Mulberry Street' Shines On." *The New York Times: Education.* The New York Times Company. 29 Jan. 2012. Web.

MICROWAVE OVEN

Bellis, Mary. "History of the Oven from Cast Iron to Electric." *ThoughtCo: Humanities, History and Culture.* ThoughtCo. 30 April 2017. Web.

Bramen, Lisa. "Cooking Through the Ages: A Timeline of Oven Inventions." *Smithsonian.com.* Smithsonian Institution. 18 Nov. 2011. Web.

Bock, Gordon. "History of the Kitchen Stove." *Old House Online.* Cruz Bay Publishing, Inc. 1 Aug. 2012. Web.

MONGOLS IN EUROPE

Marshall, Robert. *Storm From the East: From Genghis Khan to Khubilai Khan.* Berkeley: University of California Press, 1993. Print.

Spuler, Bertold. *The Mongols in History.* New York: Praeger Publishers, Inc., 1971. Print.

McLynn, Frank. *Genghis Khan: His Conquests, His Empire, His Legacy.* Boston: Da Capo Press, 2015. Print.

Burgan, Michael. *Empire of the Mongols: Great Empires of the Past.* New York: Facts on Fire, 2005. Print.

"The Mongol Conquests, 1200-1300 AD." New York: Time-Life Books/Time Frame Series, 1989. Print.

Timotheus. "The Mongol Invasion of Europe." *All Empires Online History Community.* All Empires. 27 March 2007. Web.

Firas. "The Mongol Invasion and the Destruction of Baghdad." *Lost Islamic History.* Lost Islamic History. 17 November 2012. Web.

"The Mongols and the Mamluks." *Islamic History.* Web.

ROLLING STONES

Sandford, Christopher. *Keith Richards: Satisfaction*. New York: Carroll & Graf Publishers, 2004. Print.

Richards, Keith. *Life*. New York: Little Brown and Company, 2010. Print.

Raj, Bert. *The Rolling Stones in the Beginning*. Buffalo: Firefly Books, 2006. Print.

rollingstones.com. Web.

Norman, Philip. *Mick Jagger*. London: Harper Collins Publishers, 2012. Print.

Anderson, Christopher. *Mick: The Wild Life and Mad Genius of Jagger*. New York: Galley Books, 2013. Print.

PENICILLIN

Markel, Dr. Howard. "The Real Story Behind Penicillin." PBS Newshour: The Rundown. NewsHour Productions LLC. 27 Sept. 2013. Web.

"Penicillin: An accidental discovery changed the course of medicine." Healio: Endocrine Today. Healio. Aug. 2008. Web.

Alharbi, Sulaiman Ali. "What if Fleming had not discovered penicillin?" Saudi Journal of Biological Sciences Vol. 21, Issue 4. Elsevier B. V. Sept. 2014. Web.

"The History of Antibiotics." HealthyChildren.org. American Academy of Pediatrics. 21 November 2015. Web.

"Medical Definition of Penicillin History." MedicineNet.com. MedicineNet, Inc. 25 Jan. 2017. Web.

"Alexander Fleming." *Research Begins Here: New World Encyclopedia*. New World Encyclopedia. 1 Nov. 2013. Web.

"Answers to your Civil War Questions." *Civil War Trust*. Civil War Trust. 2017. Web.

GEORGE HALAS

Cheatham, Marion. "Everyday Eastland." *ChicagoNow*. Chicago Tribune. 28 July 2014. Web.

Davis, Jeff. *Papa Bear: The Life and Legacy of George Halas*. New York: McGraw-Hill, 2005. Print.

Whittingham, Richard. *The Bears: A 75-Year Celebration*. Dallas: Taylor Publishing, 1994. Print.

Hodge, Meredith. "The History." *Eastland Disaster Historical Society*. Eastland Disaster Historical Society. 2016. Web.

Gordon, Aaron. "NFL by the Numbers." *Sports on Earth*. MLB Advanced Media, L.P. 10 Dec. 2013. Web.

CORN FLAKES

"Our Best Days Are Yours." *Kellogg's: Our History*. Kellogg NA Co. 2017. Web.

Marsh, Jan. "Sex and Sexuality in the 19th Century." *Victoria & Albert Museum*. Victoria & Albert Museum. 2016. Web.

Cavendish, Richard. "The Battle of the Cornflakes." *History Today*. History Today Ltd. 2 Feb. 2006. Web.

Soniak, Matt. "Corn Flakes were invented as part of an anti-masturbation crusade." *Mental Floss*. Mental Floss, Inc. 28 December 2012. Web.

Olson, Samantha. "The Origins of Kellogg's Corn Flakes: Doctor Who Invented Them Hoped They'd Get People to Stop Masturbating." *Medical Daily*. Newsweek Media Group. 3 Aug. 2015. Web.

Pilny, Christopher. "Kellogg's Corn Flakes: The Fascinating History of Everyday Objects #2." *Dish Magazine*. Smash Media Group, Inc. 2013. Web.

Gale, Thomson. "Kellogg Company." *Encyclopedia.com*. Encyclopedia.com. 2006. Web.

"Breakfast Cereal Statistics." *Statistic Brain*. Statistic Brain Research Institute. 2016. Web.

MCCLELLAN

McPherson, James M. Bruce Catton, narrative. *The American Heritage New History of the Civil War*. New York: Viking Press, 1996. Print.

Weigley, Russell F. *A Great Civil War: A Military and Political History 1861-1865*. Bloomington: Indiana University Press, 2000. Print.

McPherson, James M. *Crossroads of Freedom: Antietam and the Battle That Changed the Course of the Civil War.* Oxford: Oxford University Press, 2002. Print.

Jones, Wilbur D. "Who Lost the Lost Order?: Stonewall Jackson, His Courier, and Special Order No. 191" (reprinted from Civil War Regiments: A Journal of the American Civil War, Vol. 5, No. 3, 1997). *Reocities.* Reocities. Web.

MONGOLS IN JAPAN

"Kamikaze of 1274 and 1281." *Encyclopaedia Brittanica.* Encyclopaedia Brittanica, Inc. 18 Nov. 20116. Web.

Powell, Devin. "Japan's Kamikazi Winds, the Stuff of Legend, May Have Been Real." *National Geographic.* National Geographic Partners, LLC. 15 Nov. 2014. Web.

Grousset, Rene, translated by Naomi Walford. *The Empire of the Steppes: A History of Central Asia.* New Brunswick: Rutgers University Press, 1970. Print.

CONSTANTINE AND THE COMET

Whitehouse, David. "Space Impact 'saved Christianity.'" *BBC News.* BBC. 23 June 2003. Web.

Stephenson, Paul. *Constantine: Roman Emperor, Christian Victor.* New York: Overlook Press, 2010. Print.

Cary, M. and Scullard, H. H. *A History of Rome Down to the Reign of Constantine.* 3rd ed. New York: St. Martin's Press, 1975. Print.

Steel, Duncan. "The day the sky fell in." *The Guardian.* Guardian News and Media Limited. 5 Feb. 2003. Web.

HANDEL

cpr.org "George Frideric Handel and His Life-Saving Coat Button." Jean Inaba February 19, 2015. Web.

Interlude.hk "Saved by 'Cleopatra': Handel-Mattheson Duel." Georg Predota. 20 July 2014. Web.

newyorker.com "En Garde." Arthur Krystal. 12 March 2007. Web.

"The History of Dueling in America." *WTTW: American Experience.* PBS Online/WGBH. 2000. Web.

geriwalton.com "Pistol Dueling, Its Etiquette and Rules." Geri Walton. 1 August 2014. Web.

MARK TWAIN

Twain, Mark. "How I Escaped Being Killed in a Duel." *Twain Harte Visitor Guide.* Yosemite North Vistor Guide. 12 Dec. 1872. Web.

Clifton, Guy. "An Artifact of Mark Twain's 'Duel That Never Was.'" *Reno Gazette Journal.* USA Today Network. 19 Dec. 2014. Web.

"Mark Twain/A Young Journalist and a Virginia City Duel." *Trips Into History/Historic Sites.* Trips Into History. 14 Aug. 2012. Web.

"The Comstock Lode and the Mining Frontier." *Digital History.* Digital History. 2016. Web.

Powers, Ron. *Mark Twain: A Life.* New York: Free Press, 2005. Print.

Lauber, John. *The Making of Mark Twain: A Biography.* Boston: Houghlin Mifflin, 1985. Print.

ABRAHAM LINCOLN

"Man Knowledge: Dueling Part II—Prominent Duels in American History." *The Art of Manliness.* The Art of Manliness. 20 Mar. 2010, updated 4 Dec. 2015. Web.

Johnson, Kelsey. "Abraham Lincoln's Duel and Broadswords and Banks." *Civil War Trust.* Civil War Trust. 2017. Web.

Donald, David Herbert. *Lincoln.* New York: Simon and Schuster, 1995. Print.

"The History of Dueling in America." *WTTW: American Experience.* PBS Online/WGBH. 2000. Web.

ACCIDENTAL INVENTIONS: FOOD EDITION

"Ruth Wakefield: Chocolate Chip Cookie Inventor." *Famous Women Inventors.* Famous Women Inventors. 2008. Web.

Krake, Kate. "The Accidental Invention of the Chocolate Chip Cookie." *Today I Found Out: Feed Your Brain.* Disqus. 15 Mar. 2013. Web.

Michaud, Jon. "Sweet Morsels: A History of the Chocolate Chip Cookie." *The New Yorker: Culture Desk.* Conde Nast. 19 Dec. 2003. Web.

"Potato Chip History: Invention of the Potato Chip." *The Great Idea Finder.* The Great Idea Finder. 20 April 2007. Web.

Lee, Tanya H. "The Secret History of Potato Chips." *Indian Country Today.* Indian County Today Media Network. 27 Jan. 2017. Web.

Blitz, Matt. "The Truth About the Origin of the Potato Chip." *Today I Found Out: Feed Your Brain.* Disqus. 11 Sept. 2014. Web.

"Crispy Potato Chips Invented in Saratoga." *Saratoga.com.* Saratoga.com. 2017. Web.

"The History of the Ice Cream Cone." *International Dairy Foods Association: Making a Difference for Dairy.* International Dairy Foods Association. Web.

"History of the Ice Cream Cone." *What's Cooking America.* What's Cooking America. Web.

Fabry, Merrill. "The Murky History of the Ice Cream Cone." *TIME History.* Time, Inc. 12 April 2016. Web.

Moss, Robert. "The 1904 World's Fair: A Turning Point for American Food." *Serious Eats.* Serious Eats Inc. Web.

McConnell, Ericka. "The History of Popsicles." *Country Living.* Hearst Communications, Inc. 20 May 2010. Web.

Pope, Shelby. "How an 11-year-old Boy Invented the Popsicle." *The Salt: What's on Your Plate.* National Public Radio. 22 July 2015. Web.

Fiegl, Amanda. "A Brief History of Popsicles." *Smithsonian.com.* Smithsonian Institution. 7 July 2010. Web.

"History of Saccharin." *Saccharin.* Calorie Control Council. 2016. Web.

Smallwood, Karl. "The Accidental Discovery of Saccharin, and the Truth About Whether Saccharin is Bad for You." *Today I Found Out: Feed Your Brain.* Disqus. 21 May 2014. Web.

Bilger, Burkhard. "The History of Splenda, the Best-Selling Artificial Sweetener in America." *La Leva di Archimede: Hidden Truths, News You Probably Won't Hear on TV.* Reprinted from May 2006 edition of *The New Yorker.* 6 December 2006. Web.

Accidental Inventions: Toy Edition

Miss Celania. "The Amazing Origin of Silly Putty." *Neatorama.* Neatorama. 3 May 2011. Web.

Fawcett, Kirsten. "15 Facts About Silly Putty." *Mental Floss.* Mental Floss, Inc. 15 Sept. 2015. Web.

"The Weird Accident Behind the Invention of Silly Putty." *Science 2.0: Join the Revolution.* ION Publications LLC. 9 May 2011. Web.

Fiegl, Amanda. "A Brief History of Chewing Gum." *Smithsonian.com.* Smithsonian Institution. 16 June 2009. Web.

"History of Chewing Gum." *Chewing Gum Facts.* Chewing Gum Facts. 2017. Web.

Nix. Elizabeth. "Chew on This: The History of Chewing Gum." *Hungry History.* A&E Television Networks, LLC. 12 Feb. 2015. Web.

"History of Gum." *Wrigley: About Us.* Wm. Wrigley Jr. Company. 2016. Web.

Oliver, Kristen. "The World's 13 Weirdest Gum Flavors." *The Daily Meal.* Tronc, Inc. 28 Aug. 2014. Web.

"Slinky." *National Toy Hall of Fame.* The Strong. 2017. Web.

Crockett, Zachary. "The Invention of the Slinky." *Priceonomics.* Priceonomics. 3 Dec. 2014. Web.

Bellis, Mary. "History of the Slinky Toy." *The Inventors.* The New York Times Company. 2006. Web.

Morehouse, Jay. "'Slinky' … Walking Wire Coil Brings Fame, Fortune and Headaches to Dick James, It's Discoverer." Upper Darby News. 26 Aug. 1948. Print.

Hiskey, Daven. "Play-Doh was Originally Wallpaper Cleaner." *Today I Found Out: Feed Your Brain.* Disqus. 12 Nov. 2011. Web.

"Who Invented Play-Doh?" *Wonderopolis.* National Center for Families Learning. 2017. Web.

ACCIDENTAL INVENTIONS: OTHER

Abbott, Leigh. "A History of Brandy in America." Coppers and Kings. 5 Jan. 2015. Web.

"Origin of Brandy." *Scientific American.* Scientific American, a Division of Nature America, Inc. 2017. Web.

Tom. "Brandy—An Accidental Finding That Turned Delightful." *The Thrill Society: What's Your Thrill?* The Thrill Society. 14 April 2016. Web.

"7 Amazing Benefits of Brandy." *Organic Facts.* Organic Facts. Web.

"Who Invented the Artificial Pacemaker?" *Science and Inventions.* Science and Inventions. Web.

Kelly. "Wilson Greatbatch, the Man Who Accidentally Invented the Pacemaker, Has Died." *Gizmodo.* Gizmodo Media Group. 28 Sept. 2011. Web.

Williamson, Marcus. "Wilson Greatbatch: Inventor of the implantable cardiac pacemaker." *Independent.* Independent Digital News and Media. 29 Sept. 2011. Web.

"Viagra: How a Little Blue Pill Changed the World." *Drugs.com.* Drugs.com. 26 Nov. 2016. Web.

Finkel, Rhona. "How Viagra Was Discovered." *Drugsdb.com.* Drugsdb.com. 31 July 2012. Web.

"An Idea That Stuck: How a Hymnal Bookmark Helped Inspire the Post-It Note." *Special Series: my big break.* National Public Radio. 26 July 2014. Web.

"A NOTE-able Achievement." *Post It Brand: The Whole Story.* 3M. 2017. Web.

Glass, Nick and Hume, Tim. "The 'hallelujah moment' behind the invention of the Post-It note." *CNN.* Cable News Network. 4 April 2013. Web.

"Roy J. Plunkett." *Chemical Heritage Foundation.* Chemical Heritage Foundation. 27 July 2015. Web.

Hiskey, Daven. "Teflon Was Invented by Accident." *Today I Found Out: Feed Your Brain.* Disqus. 26 Aug. 2011. Web.

"History of Super Glue." *The Original Super Glue.* Super Glue Corp. 2016. Web.

Grossman, David. "The Serendipitous History of Super Glue." *PM.* Popular Mechanics, a part of Hearst Digital Media. 6 Feb. 2017. Web.

Hiskey, David. "Super Glue Was Invented by Accident Twice." *Today I Found Out: Feed Your Brain.* Disqus. 23 Aug. 2011. Web.

Harris, Elizabeth A. "Harry Coover, Super Glue Inventor, Dies at 84." *The New York Times.* The New York Times Company. 27 Mar. 2011. Web.

"Intro to Teflon." *The Role of Chemistry in History.* The Role of Chemistry in History. 19 April 2008. Web.

STARS DISCOVERED BY CHANCE

Gerber, Jamie. "15 Stars Who Became Actors Accidentally." *Screen Rant.* Screen Rant. 25 Nov. 2016. Web.

"10 Millionaire Celebs That Were Discovered in Weird Ways." *My First Class Life.* My First Class Life. Web.

"Toni Braxton." *Billboard.* Billboard. 2017. Web.

THE TELEGRAPH

"Morse Code and the Telegraph." *History.* A&E Television Networks, LLC. 2017. Web.

"Samuel F. B. Morse." *Biography.* A&E Television Networks, LLC. 2017. Web.

Carlisle, Rodney. *Scientific American Inventions and Discoveries: All the Milestones in Ingenuity from the Discovery of Fire to the Invention of the Microwave.* Hoboken: John Wiley & Sons, Inc., 2004. Print.

WATERGATE

Buncombe, Andrew. "Chance meeting that changed political history." *Nzherald.co.nz*. NZME Publishing Limited. 4 June 2005. Web.

"The Watergate Story." *The Washington Post*. The Washington Post. 2017. Print.

Woodward, Bob. *The Secret Man: The Story of Watergate's Deep Throat*. New York: Simon & Schuster, 2005. Print.

Waldron, Lamar. *Watergate: The Hidden History: Nixon, The Mafia and The CIA*. Berkeley: Counterpoint, 2012. Print.

BERLIN WALL

McElroy, Damien. "Berlin Wall: East German spokesman admits triggering collapse of wall." *The Telegraph*. Telegraph Media Group Limited. 10 Nov. 2009. Web.

Meyer, Michael. "Gunter Schabowski, the Man Who Opened the Wall." *The New York Times*. The New York Times Company. 6 Nov. 2015. Web.

"Berlin Wall." *History*. A&E Television Networks, LLC. 2017. Web.

Taylor, Frederick. *The Berlin Wall: A World Divided, 1961-1989*. Great Britain: Bloomsbury Publishing, 2006. Print.

ADOLPH HITLER

"The Rise of Adolph Hitler: From Unknown to Dictator of Germany." *The History Place*. The History Place. 1996. Web.

"Hitler Sketches That Failed to Secure His Place in Art Academy to be Auctioned." *The Telegraph*. Telegraph Media Group Limited. 24 Mar. 2010. Web.

Trueman, C N. "Adolf Hitler." *The History Learning Site*. History Learning Site. 26 May 2015 and 16 Aug. 2016. Web.

"25 Rarely Seen Artworks Painted by Adolph Hitler." *So Bad So Good: The Best & Worst of the Web*. So Bad So Good PTY Ltd. 22 July 2013. Web.

Fest, Joachim. *Hitler*. New York: Harcourt Brace Jovanovich, 1974. Print.

Duggan, Bob. "How Vienna in 1900 Gave Birth to Modern Style and Identity." *Big Think*. The Big Think, Inc. 2017. Web.

LUCKY BREAKS

Wiseman, Richard. *The Luck Factor: The Four Essential Principals*. New York: Miramax Books, 2004. Print.

Topping, Seymour. "Biography of Joseph Pulitzer." *The Pulitzer Prizes*. The Pulitzer Prizes. 2013. Web.

"This Day in History: March 4, 1952. Ronald Reagan and Nancy Davis Marry." *History*. A&E Television Networks, LLC. 2017. Web.

Crockett, Emily. "Nancy Reagan had a fascinating life. Here are some things you may not know about her." *Vox*. Vox Media. 6 Mar. 2016. Web.

Edwards, Anne. *The Reagans: Portrait of a Marriage*. New York: St. Martins Press, 2003. Print.

Bibel, Sara. "Poof! 5 Little Known Facts About How J. K. Rowling Brought Harry Potter to Life." *Biography*. A&E Television Networks, LLC. 30 July 2014. Web.

Lawless, John. "Revealed: The eight-year-old girl who saved Harry Potter." *NZHerald.co.nz*. NZME Publishing Limited. 3 July 2005. Web.

Kirk, Connie Ann. *J.K. Rowling: A Biography*. Westport: Greenwood Press, 2003. Print.

"Lerner and Loewe Biography." *Musicianguide.com*. Net Industries. 2017. Web.

Lerner, Alan Jay. *The Street Where I Live*. New York: W.W. Norton & Company, 1978. Print.

McHugh, Dominic. *Loverly: The Life and Times of My Fair Lady*. New York: Oxford University Press, 2012. Print.

ARCHDUKE FERDINAND

Wallance, Gregory J. "The Wrong Turn That Changed a Century and Still Haunts Us Today." *Forbes.* Forbes Media LLC. 27 June 2014. Web.

Reese, Byron. "One Wrong Turn and a Hundred Million People Die." *Byron Reese.* Byron Reese. 1 Nov. 2011. Web.

Dash, Mike. "Curses: Archduke Ferdinand and His Astounding Death Car." *Smithsonian.com.* Smithsonian Institution. 22 April 2013. Web.

Keegan, John. *The First World War.* New York: Alfred Knopf, 1999. Print.

Hart, Peter. *The Great War: A Combat History of the First World War.* Great Britain: Oxford University Press, 2013. Print.

EARTH AND SKY

Martisiute, Laura. "Archaeological Discoveries That Were Made by Pure Chance." *Listverse.* Listverse Ltd. 17 June 2016. Web.

Scoles, Sarah. "Oops! 8 Discoveries Astronomers Didn't Mean to Make." *Discover: Science for the Curious.* Kalmbach Publishing Co. 10 February 2015. Web.

Wayman, Erin. "Five Accidental Hominid Fossil Discoveries." *Smithsonian.com.* Smithsonian Institution. 22 Aug. 2012. Web.

"Accidental Archaeological Discoveries: Photos." *Seeker.* Seeker. 12 Dec. 2012. Web.

Black, John. "Accidental Discovery of 8,000-year-old Settlement and Necropolis in Greece." *Ancient Origins: Reconstructing the Story of Humanity's Past.* Ancient Origins. 16 April 2014. Web.

Flood, Rebecca. "Man accidentally discovers a perfectly preserved Roman villa in his backyard." *Independent.* Independent Digital News & Media. 17 Apr. 2016. Web.

Kilgrove, Kristina. "Roman Villa Mosaics Inspired These Gorgeous Archaeological Rugs." *Forbes.* Forbes Media LLC. 22 Apr. 2016. Web.

"Understanding Science: The story of serendipity." *Understanding Science: How Science Really Works.* University of California Museum of Paleontology. Web.

"The Accidental Discovery of an Underground World." *Fossil HD.* Fossil HD. 4 Dec. 2011. Web.

CHARLES GOODYEAR

"Charles Goodyear: Inventor of Vulcanized Rubber." *American Inventors.* American Inventors. 2010. Web.

"The Charles Goodyear Story." *Goodyear Corporate.* The Goodyear Rubber & Tire Company. Reprinted from the Readers Digest, January 1958 issue. 2017. Web.

Wolf, Ralph F. *India Rubber Man.* Caldwell, Idaho: The Caxton Printers, Ltd., 1940. Print.

FAMOUS PEOPLE WHO ELUDED DEATH

"Over 350 Passengers Canceled Their Reservations or Didn't Show Up for the Hijacked 9/11 Flights." *Shoestring 9/11.* Shoestring 9/11. 22 Aug. 2014. Web.

Weidinger, Patrick. "10 Famous People Who Avoided Death on 9/11." *Listverse.* Listverse Ltd. 12 Dec. 2011. Web.

Weiss, Mathew Cole. "13 People Who Narrowly Escaped Death on 9/11." *Ranker: Vote on Everything.* Ranker. Web.

Daughtery, Greg. "8 Famous People Who Missed the Lusitania." *Smithsonian.com.* Smithsonian Institution. 1 May 2013. Web.

Betts, Stephen L. "Flashback: How Waylon Jennings Survived the Day the Music Died." *Rolling Stone.* Rolling Stone Magazine. 3 Feb. 2015. Web.

Mohoney, Gillian. "Dutch Cyclist Avoids Tragedy After Being Scheduled on Two Doomed Flights." *ABC News.* Yahoo-ABC News Network. 19 July 2014. Web.

Withnall, Adam. "Dutch Cyclist Maarten de Jonge Cheats Death Twice After Changing Flights from Both Malaysia Airlines MH17 and MH370." *Independent.* Independent Digital News and Media. 20 July 2014. Web.

71140804R00062

Made in the USA
Lexington, KY
18 November 2017